EVIDENCE FOR CREATION

Intelligent answers for open minds

Tom DeRosa

Evidence for Creation:
Intelligent answers for open minds

Tom DeRosa

Third edition, first printing: 2015

ISBN 978-1-921643-92-7

Published by:

CREATION BOOK PUBLISHERS

Creation Book Publishers
P.O. Box 350
Powder Springs, GA, 30127, USA.
Phone: 1-800-616-1264
creationbookpublishers.com

CONTENTS

Introduction

by Philip Bell

THIS BOOK REALLY DOES LIVE UP TO ITS TITLE'S CLAIM, TO PROVIDE SCIENTIFIC answers to the age-old question of origins. But the caveat in the title—for *open* minds—is a crucial one. There is often a pretence of open-mindedness, but far too many people in our modern scientific age are unprepared even to give the case for biblical Creation a hearing.

In recent years the USA has witnessed appeals to the judiciary to rule Intelligent Design (ID) as anti-science. Elsewhere, governments have introduced measures to restrict the airing of alternatives to evolution in school classrooms. Legislation passed in the UK sanctions the discussion of ID and creationism in religious education classes, as long as 'evidence-based' views are excluded—a gagging order if there ever was one! Supposedly, teenagers who are studying for their public examinations in science are too inexperienced to be able to properly assess the competing views about origins. Exposing young people to such information is merely calculated to 'confuse their impressionable minds', or so it is claimed. And as if that were not all, we are repeatedly told that evolution is an established scientific theory; that alternative viewpoints are not science and, thus, are 'justifiably' outlawed.

Consensus science?

The secular authorities, supported by a biased and sometimes mendacious media, are at pains to inform us that this position is entirely reasonable because it represents the established scientific consensus. Yet, for those prepared to acknowledge it, there's a massive disconnect between the behaviour of these 'powers that be' and their plea to be balanced, fair and open-minded. The history of science bears witness to the way in which, all too often, a consensus mentality hindered significant advance in one field or another. Some who are hailed as great scientists today were only given their due recognition posthumously; in life their efforts were rewarded with marginalisation and opposition in equal measure. Gratifyingly, others who dared to challenge the consensus of their day made real breakthroughs which were recognised during their lifetimes, so enjoyed the fruit of their labour.

On the issue of origins, the ruling paradigm has long been that of molecules-to-man evolution. Those men and women of science who, defying the consensus view, have been prepared to stick their heads above the parapet deserve our applause. Whether in the fields of cosmology and physics, the earth sciences, the life sciences or anthropology, their labours are bearing much fruit. The evidence which they have amassed in support of Creation is the subject of this book.

Beyond Intelligent Design

But the author does not stop there, unashamedly declaring the identity of the Designing Deity who is responsible for Creation—the infinitely intelligent God of the Bible. For those who truly have open minds, the evidence from these many and varied facets of science points unambiguously to the Creator, Jesus Christ. It is surely safe to conclude that the Apostle Paul would have warmly commended scientific endeavours done from the perspective of this biblical worldview. He taught that the attributes and qualities of the Creator are so "clearly revealed" as to render all *naturalistic* philosophical thinking inexcusable (Romans 1:20).

Where does that leave those theistic evolutionists who explicitly, even vehemently, decry Intelligent Design as unscientific? Their god would seem to be little different from the Deists' god, barred from the responsibility of having *designed* what we observe, or from having done it *intelligently*. Are we seriously to conclude that they would have us believe in the *unintelligent* creation of merely *apparent* designs? For this would seem to be practically synonymous with the doctrine long espoused by Darwinian 'high priest' Richard Dawkins and other evolutionist aficionados.

Where open-mindedness should lead

Tom DeRosa's short book deftly and insightfully explores information from a wealth of sources with the aim of instilling truth into open-minded readers. In our morally degraded and increasingly godless western societies, these intelligent answers helpfully reveal where the battle is really at. The creation/evolution debate, and allied controversies over the age of the earth, can be distilled down to arguments over authority. On one hand, advocates of moral relativism insist that man is his own authority, this in turn being the legitimate child of secular humanism. On the other hand, traditional Christian morality and ethics flow readily from an acceptance of the Bible as God's authoritative Word. Such Christian values lack any logical connection with the conception of origins arising from the neoDarwinian worldview.

More than a century and a half has elapsed since Darwin unveiled his evolutionary theory. Were he somehow able to see our day, one wonders what he would make of his native Britain and other countries which have eagerly embraced his ideas. Sexual promiscuity, soaring divorce rates, record levels of child abuse, family meltdown and other social ills have become the norm. Crime rates are putting police forces under increasing pressure, so that the solving of 'petty crimes' (such as car thefts[1]) is increasingly seen as the victim's responsibility. Alarm has been expressed by the *World Health Organisation* that suicide globally is now the second leading cause of death in 15-29 year olds, with governments being urged to tackle the problem.[2]

It would be over-simplistic to lay the blame for all these societal ills at the door of evolutionary belief. Nevertheless, the latter has doubtless been a significant contributor. Generations of people have been taught (from an increasingly young age) that they are merely rearranged pond scum, and that there is no accountability to a Loving Creator God. The book in your hands is an antidote to this pernicious lie. May it be wonderfully used to provide intelligent answers, even leading some readers to saving faith in our great Creator and Saviour, the Lord Jesus Christ.

Philip Bell
BSc(Hons) Zoology; PGCE; CBiol MSB
CEO, Creation Ministries International–UK/*Europe*

Notes

1. For example, Policing report: Victims 'asked to investigate crime themselves', bbc.co.uk/news, 4 September 2014.
2. Preventing suicide: a global imperative, W.H.O., September 2014, who.int/mental_health/suicide-prevention/world_report_2014/en.

Chapter One

Evidence for What?

Crime scene evidence is extremely important. A skillful detective can use fingerprints, DNA, clothing fibers, etc., to recreate the crime and identify the perpetrator. Our legal system also relies on evidence. The law defines evidence as 'material objects and verbal statements admissible at trial'. In a more general sense, evidence, when properly used, leads to the right conclusion or to a judgment that brings one to the truth.

In the origins debate, the evidence leads to one of two conclusions: evolution or creation. These two basic views are completely at odds and admit no middle ground. On the one hand, evolution relies on pure random chance as the agent by which matter and energy, over time, are assembled into living systems with all their mind-boggling complexity. The evolutionary process, we are told, requires billions and billions of years. Creation, by contrast, relies on the 'mechanism' of an outside intelligence which we define as the Creator, the One who made from nothing a universe exhibiting order and design. Vast stretches of time are not needed for creation.

> The evidence leads to one of two conclusions: evolution or creation.

The evolution/creation debate centers on events in the past. It is an inquiry that seeks to detect and assemble evidence, just as a detective investigates a crime scene.

In both cases, the evidence collected will introduce clues to help us understand what happened in the past. As in a court of law, the evidence used in the origins debate can be verbal or material. That evidence must be qualified and have integrity so that it will be admissible to all who are in a position to make a judgment. Because there is a danger that the final verdict will be erroneous, if based on falsified evidence, the evidence submitted must be highly reliable to make its conclusions compelling to all who examine it with an open mind.

The evidence is employed by both sides. In the origins debate, both the advocates of creation and of evolution rely on the same physical evidence to prove their case. The origins debate is unique because it seeks to explain a one-time event. Therefore, historical data are relied on for clues as to what happened. Evidence from rocks, bones, stars, and living systems are interpreted to understand what happened in the past. The acquisition, processing, and analysis of evidence is always subject to error, and since no human was present to observe the origin of life, there is no verbal evidence of how everything came to be. How, after all, could we observe the big bang or see firsthand as God created the universe? The only way to understand these one-time events in the past is to sift through the evidence left behind—just like a detective at a crime scene.

Here are some important ideas to remember, as you consider the evidence:

1. Both sides use evidence.
2. We are limited in our capacity to assess the evidence. We are finite, biased, sinful, and unable to revisit the past to witness what took place at creation.
3. The creation/evolution debate is an historical inquiry that examines material and verbal evidence. The material evidence includes:
    a. The fossil record
    b. Geological formations
    c. Complexity of living systems
    d. Biological molecular structures/DNA
    e. Astronomical objects
    f. Light from astronomical objects
4. The verbal evidence is contained in the Genesis account in the Bible, the Word of God.

Why does the same evidence lead to opposite conclusions?

Advocates of evolution and creation use the same evidence, but come to different conclusions. Why? When a fossilized dinosaur bone is discovered, the evolutionist will immediately interpret it as the consequence of eons of death and suffering that ultimately led to the dinosaur's extinction. The creationist, however, understands that fossil as evidence of a worldwide flood that created the chemical and physical conditions for fossil formation. This pattern is repeated time after time as the same evidence leads to opposite conclusions. The evidence is acquired with meticulous care and treated with the same scientific tools. Accurate measurements are made and analyzed; yet, at the end of the discovery process, there are two very different conclusions.

The reason for this is that both sides approach the evidence with opposite presuppositions or preconceptions. When evidence is presented in a court of law, the goal is to produce a verdict of guilt or innocence. The advocates on each side enter the courtroom with their minds made up. The prosecutor is looking for a guilty verdict and uses the evidence to persuade the court to that end. The defense builds a case for innocence, also, by using the evidence. It is important to acknowledge that both prosecutor and defender come to court with preconceptions. They presuppose their conclusions from the same set of data.

Likewise, defenders of evolution or creation look at the data in terms of their bias. Creationists, who use the Word of God to establish their presuppositions about the origin of life, reach dramatically different conclusions than do those who reject the Bible as a record of the past. Contrasting presuppositions always produce contrasting conclusions. Take a look at the presuppositions both sides bring to the origins question:

Creation	Evolution
Predetermined Order	Chaos
Outside Intelligence	Internal Self Ordering
Six Days	Millions of Years
Catastrophic Events	Slow Gradual Change

In Badlands National Park, located in southwestern South Dakota, the world's richest fossil beds which evolutionists assign to the Oligocene epoch are found.

Badlands National Park, SD

The evolutionists who study these fossil beds conclude that over 12 million years of mammalian evolution took place. They approach these fossil sites with the presupposition that evolution is a fact, and therefore, come to a conclusion that all the different fossilized forms came to be by the process of gradual change over millions and millions of years. With the same fossil evidence that the evolutionists use, creationists reach very different conclusions. They find evidence of different kinds of mammals and propose that the layering of rocks and fossils was due to some sort of catastrophic event, such as a worldwide flood. Again, we find two competing conclusions from the same evidence. It comes down to one's presuppositions, or worldview.

Worldviews at war

The evolution/creation debate has been around for a long time. It flared up in the nineteenth century after the publication of Charles Darwin's *Origin of Species,* which quickly became popular in England and spread across Europe. Many believe that Darwin discovered evolution. In reality, its roots can be traced to the prehistoric confrontation between men and their Creator. According to Henry Morris, a scientist and author widely considered to be the father of the modern creation movement, Darwin happened along at the right historical moment to spark a movement that was really just the renewal of an ancient idea:

> The fact is, however, he really only served as the catalyst for revival of ancient paganism, coming at just the right time in history to bring to fruition a revolt against God for which many in Western Europe had been preparing for over a century.[1]

Evolution, since Darwin, has gradually taken over Western culture. Today, it has taken root in all major academic disciplines. Sadly, some church bodies have subscribed to evolution in some form or fashion, evidently not understanding evolution's atheistic premise. Churches accept evolution because it comes dressed in the garb of scientific authority but, in fact, it is a movement whose main thrust is to do away with God. Evolution has gained such acceptance in higher education that it is regarded by many elites in education and the media as the only intellectual option. It has become an accepted worldview.

> Opposite worldviews lead to opposite presuppositions in the evolution/creation debate.

A worldview may be defined as a framework for understanding reality. It is that set of core beliefs by which knowledge is filtered, decisions made, values established, and priorities set. Every human being, young or old, has within himself a worldview. It is nurtured in childhood and adolescence and grows ever more deeply ingrained with age. Worldviews can, however, dramatically change as, for example, when an individual is born again and becomes, as the Bible puts it, "a new creature in Christ." Those who encounter Christ and commit themselves to the Word of God experience a transformation that often radically alters their worldview.

A creationist worldview starts with belief in God, the Creator of all things. It is centered on the inspired Word of God that provides an account of the beginning of the universe and of man. It also supplies an early history of the world in the first eleven chapters of Genesis. It characterizes creation as "very good" in Genesis 1. In Genesis 3 it describes the Fall of man and the ramifications that are observed in a world placed under God's curse. Genesis records a great judgment in chapter 6, the worldwide flood that produces effects that influence the way the world appears today. The establishment of different nations with unique languages and cultures is recorded in Genesis 10–11. The events recorded in Genesis 1–11 form the creationist worldview and demonstrate man's accountability to his Creator.

The evolutionist worldview, by contrast, has no place for God. Evolutionists regard the universe as self-creating, with eternal matter and energy. Some evolutionists briefly acknowledge God as the great initiator who, after starting time, space, and matter, stepped away to simply let natural law take over. In the evolutionist worldview, man is in control of his destiny and basically good—the latter an idea that sharply departs from the Christian concept that man is a fallen, sinful creature saved only by God's grace. The evolutionist worldview has no moral absolutes, because all things are believed to change with time as evolution progresses. According to the Christian worldview, however, moral absolutes are part of the structure of reality as created by God.

Creationist Worldview	Evolutionist Worldview
Based on God's Word	Based on Man's Word
Creator/Outside Intelligence	Unknown Internal Process
Absolutes	Relativism
Accountability to God	Accountability to Man

Is evolution a scientific fact?

Our everyday lives revolve around science and technology. The cars we drive, the food we eat, and the vitamins we take are the result of the application of some scientific principle. Just as science is important to everyday life, so it sets foundational principles by which evidence is acquired, analyzed, and transmitted.

> Evolution is widely accepted as indisputable fact when, in truth, it is a belief system.

Science is a process in which we procure knowledge from empirical data. The data are from what we observe and record with our senses. Science is a systematic study of the world around us, based on observations, classifications, and descriptions that can lead to experimental investigation and theoretical explanations. Both deductive and inductive reasoning are employed in the scientific process. The National Academy of Science in the 1998 publication, *Teaching about Evolution and the Nature of Science,* confines the activity of science to empirical evidence, stating: "Explanations that cannot be based on empirical evidence are not a part of science."[2]

Valid science must have integrity, dependability, reliability, and be trustworthy. How can you come to true conclusions when experimental data is falsified? Testing and measuring are also important tools for verification. When scientific research is reported in scientific journals, it should be written so that experimental procedures can be repeated, since repeatability is another tool used for verification.

Science relies on observation, fact, hypothesis, theory, and law. These can be defined, briefly as follows.

Observations:	Describing or measuring what one senses.
Fact:	Based on repeated observations that can be confirmed.
Hypothesis:	A statement that can be tested so that inferences and conclusions can be explained.
Theory:	A general explanation into which facts and experimental conclusions can be incorporated, so as to allow for predictions to be made.
Law:	A functional generalization that has stood the test of time and can be relied on to make accurate predictions.

Creationists and evolutionists do science the same way—with one very important exception. Creation scientists bring to their investigation the presupposition, based on God's Word, that man is finite and fallible and in need of the revelation contained in God's Word. Along with evolutionists, the creationist agrees on the importance of peer review and self correction by means of the scientific process detailed above. However, the two camps differ, because the creationist brings to his scientific endeavor a belief in the absolute truth of the Word of God.

Science, by definition, investigates the natural world. It is not a worldview. By itself, science is a neutral mechanism that gives us tools to acquire and examine evidence. Both creationists and evolutionists depend on science to acquire, analyze, and transmit data to build working models to support theories and laws. The textbook, *Biology*, points out that:

> The raw materials of science are our observations of the phenomena of the natural universe. Science—unlike art, religion, or philosophy—is limited to what is observable and measurable and, in this sense, is roughly categorized as materialistic.[3]

Yet while science is concerned with natural objects, it does not exclude other realities. Science is a tool that gives a glimpse of truth. It is limited because it ignores man's inner spirit, motivations, and goals. It fails desperately in defining inner qualities, such as truthfulness, generosity, and love. Man's spiritual nature—the repository of his faith, convictions, and worldview—is not susceptible to scientific inquiry. Science's reality is the material world only. It is not competent to reach conclusions about realms beyond.

Science, however, is not naturalism. Naturalism is a belief system that states that all truth can be found only through empirical data—by the investigation of the material universe. Naturalism eliminates God, the Bible, and the spiritual nature of man. Only what can be observed in the material world is said to bring us to ultimate truth. Naturalism can be classified as a worldview, because it is a framework for understanding reality that arises not from observation but from *a priori* conviction about what is real (the material universe) and what is not real (God). Naturalism is the philosophical underpinning to evolution—one which evolution assumes but cannot prove. Nor does it make the attempt. Rather, naturalism is simply adopted, without evidence or argument, as the self-evidently correct worldview.

Evolutionists hold tenaciously to this belief system because it is so necessary and congenial to the idea of upward and gradual change from atoms and molecules to complex living systems. Naturalism supports the evolutionist idea that random mechanisms, without a plan or outside intelligence, assembled reality. It eliminates the work of God and is implicitly atheistic.

> Naturalism does not explicitly deny the mere existence of God, but it does deny that a supernatural being could in any way influence natural events, such as evolution, or communicate with natural creatures like ourselves. Scientific naturalism makes the same point by starting with the assumption that science, which studies only the natural, is our only reliable path to knowledge. A God who can never do anything that makes a difference, and of whom we can have no reliable knowledge, is of no importance to us.[4]

Evolution disguised as science promotes the religion of naturalism, an idea which, when applied, has led to horrible pain, suffering, and the death of millions, as will be demonstrated in chapter five. Also, this is covered in more depth in my book, *Evolution's Fatal Fruit*.[5]

The basic ideas

In summary, it is important to remember the following about evolutionary presuppositions. First, evolution assumes slow and gradual change over unimaginable eons—millions of years for life and billions of years for the heavenly universe. Many different explanations, without consensus, are offered to explain how this process took place. Second, evolution assumes that the organizing force for life is internal and depends on random chance—a presupposition that eliminates any outside intelligent creative force. Third, evolution dismisses intelligence and assumes random chance to be the mechanism responsible for material reality—a philosophical presupposition that is not drawn from empirical evidence. Evolution, therefore, is an irrational belief. It assumes randomness and chance, not design, to be the governing principle of reality, a view, again, without hard empirical data to support it.

The basic premise of creationism is that all living and nonliving systems have their origins from an outside source with infinite intelligence. This infinite intelligence is referred to as Christ the Creator, the One who spoke everything into existence. Long periods of time are not needed. The events of creation are recorded in the Bible's Genesis account. The physical evidence indicates that the cosmos is the work of an intelligent designer and planner. Creation, again, is a unique event that cannot be repeated and therefore cannot be observed in the present. Finally, creation, because it relies on an intelligent Creator, is a rational belief that presupposes the existence of a Creator God.

Is science compatible with the Bible?

Thomas Huxley

It is a popular notion that science and the Bible are at odds with one another. The rumor of warfare between the Bible and science can be traced to Thomas Huxley, a late nineteenth century apologist for evolution, who became known as Darwin's 'bull dog' and helped mightily to overthrow the cultural dominance of Christianity. But Huxley, and a long line of successors who have touted Huxley's mischievous misconception about faith and reason, are at odds with the facts of history.

The truth is that science and Christianity had a great relationship from 1500 to the late 1800s. The early pioneers of modern science had no difficulty in believing in God as their Creator and Savior. They believed in a God who had limitless power and was the source of all intelligence. The works of His hands were worthy to be studied, and to do so was to glorify Him. Indeed, Psalm 111:2 tells us that "Great are the works of the Lord, studied by all who delight in them." God affirms

Francis Bacon

the character of creation in Genesis 1 by calling it "good" five times during the week of creation. Finally, when creation is complete, He pronounces His final judgment: It is "very good."

Francis Bacon, who is often regarded as the father of the scientific method, said,

> If one considers the matter rightly, Natural Philosophy [the study of nature] is, after God's Word, the surest medicine for superstition, and also the most approved nourishment of Faith. And so she is rightly given to Religion as a most faithful handmaiden; the one manifesting the will of God, the other His power.[6]

Early scientists knew that by doing exhaustive research in a particular area of science, they would be fulfilling the great Cultural Mandate, taking dominion of God's creation as commanded in Genesis 1:28. This is demonstrated by a few examples from great men of science who also embraced belief in God. Henry Morris, in *Men of Science: Men of God*, lists over 40 great scientists who were professing Christians that believed in the divine authority of God. Among them are:

Johannes Kepler (1571–1630), an astronomer famous for his exhaustive work on planetary motion. He said:

> I give you thanks, Creator God, that you have given me this joy in I give you thanks, Creator God, that you have given me this joy in Thy creation, and I rejoice in the works of Your hands. See I have now completed the work to which I was called. In it I have used all the talents You have lent to my spirit.[7]

Blaise Pascal (1623–1662), a great philosopher and mathematician who is considered the father of the science of hydrostatics. He developed the principles of the barometer. Pascal's famous wager demonstrates his commitment to Christianity. His wager illustrates that Christian faith is a 'win-win' proposition. If a Christian dies and there is no God, "he has lost nothing." But if a Christian dies and there is a God, heaven, and hell, he has gained everything while "his skeptical friend has lost everything in hell."[8]

Robert Boyle (1627–1691) is considered the father of physical chemistry, with his monumental work on the mechanistic principles of gases, from which his famous Boyle's Law was generated. His experimental approach to gasses laid the foundation for atomic theory. Boyle was a devout Christian who had an interest in missions and apologetics. He was famous for his lectures in which he promoted creation as God's finely tuned clock, "where all things are so skillfully contrived that the engine being once set a-moving, all things proceed according to the Artificer's first design."[9]

John Ray (1627–1705), a botanist who introduced the first definition of species as being from reproduction. His definition, that parents produce offspring with the same kind of characteristics, is close to the modern definition. He was motivated by Genesis 1 which speaks of "plants yielding seed according to their own kinds" (v. 12). He wrote *The Wisdom of God Manifested in the Works of the Creation*, which had a great impact and "argued that living things are so complex and so marvelously designed that they must be the creation of a supremely intelligent Creator."[10]

Isaac Newton (1642–1727), known as one of the greatest scientists of all time, developed the law of universal gravitation, the laws of motion, and calculus into a branch of mathematics. He produced a particle theory to explain how light is emitted and built the first reflecting telescope. Newton understood that the creation came from God, and his basic motivation was to promote a belief in God the Creator. Newton contributed greatly to the foundations of science and believed that God was the ultimate cause.

> We account the Scriptures of God to be the most sublime philosophy. I find more sure marks of authenticity in the Bible than in any profane history whatsoever.[11]

Carl Linnaeus (1707–1778) discovered biological taxonomy, which is a classification system still used today. He classified living organisms, using species as the basic unit, based on the biblical idea that organisms do not change with time. He was a committed creationist who believed that God's creation was good and stable. Linnaeus was on the right path, and although he initially confused 'species' with 'kind,' he later recognized that several 'species' could belong to a single 'kind'. He wrote essays on natural theology in support of the idea that man can glorify God by studying His works of creation.

Follow the evidence with an open mind.

There are overwhelming testimonies from those who approached the evidence with an open mind and, as a result, started to question the worldview of naturalism. No matter from what perspective they studied the evidence, whether at the molecular level or by gazing at the heavenly bodies, they discovered evidence of a plan and a design. When they freed themselves from the chains of the religion of naturalism and followed the evidence, the mechanism of evolution was abandoned. Both the biblical creationist movement and the modern Intelligent Design movement have enlisted established scientists who are challenging, with some success, the whole evolutionary thesis.

> The evidence should bring one to a creationist worldview because the universe is the work of the infinite, intelligent God.

There is no shortage of compelling evidence to lead one to the verdict that God is the Creator. In Romans 1, Paul states that evidence for God's creative work in the world "is plain to them" (v. 19) and is "clearly perceived" (v. 20). This indicates that God reveals something of Himself through His creative work. The evidence for God from nature is so compelling, in fact, that people "are without excuse" in denying God (v. 20). The Scripture affirms that a view of the evidence without the bondage of naturalism frees man to see God the Creator.

That is not enough. God the Creator is also God our Savior. The Apostle John opens his gospel with the declaration that "In the beginning was the Word, and the Word was with God, and the Word was God." The Gospel of John begins just as Genesis 1, with the three words, "In the beginning." In Genesis 1:3, God states, "Let there be light." In John, the "Word" is not only the Creator, but the Word made flesh—Jesus Christ, the source of life and light, the One who brings everlasting life. Genesis 1 and John 1 demonstrate a link between God our Creator and God (Jesus Christ) our Savior. The examination of the evidence for creation should not just bring one to recognize God as Maker, but also bring the honest inquirer to a personal relationship with Christ his Savior, the life and light of the world.

Notes

1. Henry Morris, *The Long War Against God*, Baker Book House, Grand Rapids, 1989, p. 151.
2. *Teaching about Evolution and the Nature of Science*, Washington, D.C., National Academy Press, p. 27.
3. Helena Curtis and N. Sue Barnes, *Biology*, Worth Publishers, Inc., New York, 1989, p. 17.
4. Phillip E. Johnson, *Darwin on Trial*, InterVarsity Press, Downers Grove, Illinois, 1991, p. 115.
5. Tom DeRosa, *Evolution's Fatal Fruit*, Coral Ridge Ministries, Fort Lauderdale, Florida, 2006.
6. Francis Bacon, *Novum Organum* (1620), Bk I, Aph 89 (transl.), accessed at fbrt.org.uk/pages/quotes/quotes/quotes-divinity-philosophy.html.
7. Nancy R. Pearcey and Charles B. Thaxton, *The Soul of Science*, Crossway Books, Wheaton, Illinois, 1994, p. 23.
8. Henry Morris, *Men of Science: Men of God*, Master Books, El Cajon, California, p. 15.
9. Pearcey and Thaxton, p. 87.
10. Pearcey and Thaxton, p. 102.
11. Morris, *Men of Science: Men of God*, p. 26.

Chapter Two

Evidence from the Heavens

THE LAWS OF SCIENCE ARE THE FOUNDATION OF ALL SCIENTIFIC ENDEAVOR. They have been demonstrated to be reliable, regardless of time or place. These laws enable researchers to make accurate predictions from a given set of conditions. They demonstrate an overwhelming presence of order and design in the universe. Almost every scientific law can be expressed by means of a mathematical formula. Many are named after the scientist responsible for their discovery. Examples of these laws are listed below.

Newton's Laws of Motion	(three laws for all motion)
Universal Gravitation	(two bodies attracting each other)
Boyle's Law	(gas pressure and volume relationship)
Charles' Law	(gas temperature and volume relationships)
Ideal Gas Law	(gas temperature, volume, and pressure)
Coulomb's Law	(charges, distances between two objects)
Hooke's Law	(spring action and force)
Kepler's Law	(laws of planetary orbits)
Snell's Law	(refraction law of light)

Ohm's Law	(electrical law of volts, amps, and resistance)
Laws of Thermodynamics	(universal laws of energy and matter)

Laws suggest a lawgiver—a designer or creator of the universe. Sir Isaac Newton, the greatest scientist who ever lived, was a creationist who thought of God as the divine watchmaker. Like a fine mechanical watch, each component of creation is designed to work in harmony with every other part. This pattern of intricate coordination in the cosmos points to a creator, one who designed the universe. Newton, when developing the Law of Universal Gravitation, observed the movements of the planets around the sun, and concluded:

> This most beautiful system of sun, planets, and comets could only proceed from the counsel and dominion of an intelligent and powerful being.[1]

The laws of science are uniform, universal, and unchanging—and thus predictable. A law of science is true whether it is applied on earth, or anywhere in space. For example, Newton's laws of motion not only operate here on earth, but also on the moon or a star. No matter where you are in the universe, Newton's second law of motion predicts that whenever force is applied, a predictable acceleration will ensue. Laws of science then, are universal, repeatable, predictable, subject to mathematical expression, and evidence of order in creation.

The two great laws of science

Of all the laws of science, the laws of thermodynamics, particularly the first two, are the most important. These laws can be applied to the most enormous objects in the universe or to tiny invisible particles. They hold true for matter or energy, or both. A wide variety of conditions can be applied, and the results will always be the same. These two laws of thermodynamics impact almost every branch of science. They were formally discovered around 200 years ago in the course of experiments with heat and its movement.

The word for 'thermodynamics' comes from the Greek words 'therme', meaning heat, and 'dunamis', referring to power or energy. Energy cannot be seen and does not have mass. You can only observe its effects. You cannot see electricity, but you can see its effect when lightning strikes the earth. There are different kinds of energy—mechanical, chemical, electrical, magnetic, nuclear, heat and light. The most amazing phenomenon found while developing the steam engine during the Industrial Revolution is that heat energy can be transformed into mechanical and other kinds of energy (nuclear energy excepted). This prompted fresh insights into how all kinds of energy can be transferred from one form to another. As investigations continued, definite predictable patterns were formed. Mathematical relationships were discovered, giving birth to the most fundamental laws of science—the Laws of Thermodynamics.

Lord William T. Kelvin

These laws were developed by brilliant scientists including Lord William Thomson Kelvin (1824–1907), a devout Christian and creationist, whose stature as a scientist rivals that of Newton. Lord Kelvin made numerous contributions to science, including many inventions. He held 21 honorary doctorates. It is no surprise that he discovered these vital universal laws, given his faith that the creation came from an infinite, loving, intelligent God.

The First Law of Thermodynamics states that the amount of energy and matter remain constant. Matter or energy may change from one form to another, but will always be conserved. Matter and energy can be neither created nor destroyed. Einstein showed that they were interconvertable by his famous $E = mc^2$. This law is called the Law of Conservation of mass/energy.

The Second Law of Thermodynamics holds that energy and matter have a universal tendency to go to disorder, a process known as increase of entropy. The universe is basically running down in every form. Organization, if left alone, becomes disorganization. Energy must be added to the system to increase order and lower entropy.

Genesis and two great laws

The first two laws of thermodynamics are foundational to science because they deal with the basic stuff of the material universe—matter and energy. They apply to every living and nonliving system. The conservation of energy and matter, and the fact that a system's energy and matter are naturally running down, have great implications.

We know from the first law that matter and energy are predictable and constant. The energy input will always equal the energy output. On the other hand, the second law of disorder means that the output of *useful* energy is less than the input; the rest of the energy is wasted as heat. So work is required to keep a system going. This can be disconcerting. Machines tend to run down, living systems eventually decay and die, including humans. Even the heavenly bodies are wearing away. When one steps back to evaluate these laws and their impact on the universe, the question naturally arises as to how they came to be. Just as all laws suggest a lawgiver, so the preeminent laws of thermodynamics most assuredly had to come from the hand of God. It is irrational to believe that these universal laws exist without a foundation and for no reason. There is only one intelligent alternative: God.

> The great laws of thermodynamics originated in the Genesis account.

Genesis tells us that God completed the work of creation in six days: "Thus the heavens and the earth were finished, and all the host of them" (Genesis 2:1). All matter and energy, the earth and stars, all kinds of living creatures, including humans, were created and complete. The complete and finished work of creation indicates that all the components were in place. Nothing remained to be added or eliminated. The mass/energy could change form, but never be destroyed, as observed in the law of conservation. Whatever God created in the first week is all we have now and all we are ever going to have.

God's curse after the Fall rested not just on man for his sin, but impacted man's dominion over the earth. God told Adam that "cursed is the ground because of you" (Genesis 3:17). This is echoed by Paul in the New Testament, when he states that "the creation was subjected to futility," and that "the creation itself will be set free from its bondage to corruption" (Romans 8:20-21).

I believe that the Second Law was put into effect by God at the moment of the creation of matter and energy, because it provides avenues for energy and matter to be transferred. Water evaporation, for example, follows the Second Law, because water molecules tend to become more disordered as evaporation occurs. As you can imagine, this is important in many ways. How would you wash and dry your soiled clothes, if evaporation did not occur? One of the key parts of the Second Law is the transfer of heat energy from a hot, high-energy environment to a cold, low energy environment. Life and almost all nonliving systems need heat transfer or energy movement for their existence. The simple act of walking depends on friction, which is an application of the Second Law. Digestion means the breakdown of complex molecules in food to simpler ones that the body can reconstitute, and this is yet another example of the Second Law in action.

However, when God cursed the creation, including man, He may have removed some of His sustaining influence, for the first time allowing the second law to have a destructive impact. The curse on the world and the universe has produced dramatic and catastrophic changes.

The laws of thermodynamics and creation

When God made all things "in six days" (Exodus 20:11), He created the marvelous, intricately designed systems of the universe out of nothing. These complex created systems, too numerous to count, from small microscopic organisms to macrocosmic heavenly bodies, are all subject to the same universal law of decay. Where did this decay come from? Again, from a one-time event that must have had its origins outside the universe. It had to come from God.

> In summary, the two laws of thermodynamics indicate the necessity of some power outside present, known processes to have originally brought it all into existence. Something outside and above the vast complex of space, time, energy, material is required to have initiated it; but free from it. That is, the laws of thermodynamics can tell us that an absolute creation is necessary.[2]

The laws of thermodynamics pose a serious challenge to evolution, which assumes upward movement from simple, inert particles to complex living systems over eons of time. The observed laws demonstrate the following problems for evolution. First, since, as the First Law states, natural processes cannot add new mass/energy to the universe, where did all the matter and energy come from? Second, the system tends towards disorder—not to increase in order. So why do we have such an orderly universe?

The problem faced by evolution really lies in how a complex organism could have been built from its rudimentary component parts. Small molecules had to assemble themselves into a simple cell. That cell then had to reproduce and change until combinations of cells united together to form more complex organisms, leading eventually to human beings. But the assembly of all these living systems is extremely complicated and could not have happened by itself. An outside intelligence could bring order to the system. But molecules-to-man evolution lacks a mechanism to overcome the law of decay. (As we'll see later on, the proposed mechanism of mutation and natural selection is insufficient to reverse this tendency toward chaos.) This is a severe problem for evolution.

When you wish upon a star

The origins debate is not just confined to living things but also involves the whole cosmos. Evolution, based on naturalism, seeks to entirely exclude the idea of God. It assumes naturalistic forces to explain how the stars, sun, earth, and moon came to be. Evolutionists indulge in speculation when seeking to explain stellar, galactic, planetary, and organic evolution. Of course, evolution—which attempts to explain one-time events without any empirical data to support the theory—has never been observed. All forms of cosmology are theoretical in nature, because none can be tested. Each type of evolution above has many theories proposed for it, which suggests that there is no consensus.

Artist's conception of the Milky Way Galaxy

Heavenly bodies emit light and other radiant energies, such as radio waves, from space that can be observed across great distances. There are unimaginable distances between stellar objects. The closest star to our solar system is Alpha Centauri. It is 4.3 light years away, which is equivalent to 40.7 trillion kilometers (25.5 trillion miles), an enormous distance for a next-door neighbor. These vast distances are only multiplied when we look at our own Milky Way galaxy composed of 100 billion stars. The widest part of the Milky Way measures 120,000 light years, which is 1.1 quadrillion kilometers (696,000 trillion miles).

The vast reaches of space make the earth appear totally insignificant. The Hubble Telescope orbiting around the earth gives us ideal conditions for observing light and other radiation in space, but it still faces the problem of observable distance. The universe is composed of countless stars occupying unimaginable space. It can only be studied from a speculative, almost unrealistic position.

It is no wonder the field of cosmology has nowhere to turn but the realm of speculation. Without empirical data, it is not true science. This is exemplified by terms like 'dark matter' and 'dark energy', concepts needed, according to evolutionary cosmology, to keep things expanding and moving in the universe. The problem, however, is that they cannot be observed at present, so cosmologists are devising new instruments in hopes of finding these hidden entities. For the cosmologist, the embarrassing fact is that this unobservable and unverifiable 'dark stuff' comprises 95 percent of the universe. Only five percent is observable and can be accounted for. David Cline addressed this problem in *Scientific American*:

> Evolution of the cosmos is based primarily on speculation.

> The Universe around us is not what it appears to be. ... The motions of this visible material reveal that it is flotsam on an unseen sea of unknown material. We know little about that sea. The terms we use to describe its components, 'dark matter' and 'dark energy,' serve mainly as expressions of our ignorance.[3]

The same can be said of black holes. No one has observed one, but some have theorized that they are areas of high density to which all light is attracted. Over and over, employing speculation after speculation, evolutionary cosmology builds arguments based on specks of information that, in effect, displace the Creator God from His rightful place in His universe.

Big bang or big bust?

The big bang is the popularized version of evolutionary cosmology. It states that matter, energy, and space were all compressed many billions of times smaller than a proton and then exploded for some undetermined reason to create an expanding universe, which continues to spread today. There are presently some 50 theories proposed by cosmologists to explain the big bang, all of which are nothing but mathematical models. Why so many theories? It is apparent that the verdict is still out.

If the big bang is true, as presented by the cosmologists, they must have scientific ground to stand on. To propose that the universe came about by a big explosion has far-reaching implications that affect every human being. For cosmic evolution to be accepted, the questions below must be answered, not just with speculative theory or creative mathematical formulations, but with hard empirical evidence.

1. What causes particles of matter to coalesce into heavenly bodies?

This basic question has to be answered. If the big bang caused matter and energy to separate and move outward at tremendous speeds, at some time that matter had to coalesce and come together. The explanation offered is that as cooling occurs, particles slow down and clump together. The problem is, however, that these celestial objects are moving at relatively high speeds away from each other. There is no empirical evidence to support the star formation theory proposed by evolutionary cosmologists. No star or galaxy has ever been seen to form in space from star gas. As Harvard astrophysicist, Abraham Loeb stated, "The truth is that we don't understand star formation at a fundamental level."[4]

2. Can an explosion produce order?

The Second Law of Thermodynamics, as noted above, tends to bring a system to disorder. The cosmos is not exempt from the Second Law. When one observes the universe, the Second Law is apparent everywhere. The sun is wearing down slowly; stars are burning out and even exploding. It is obvious that the Second Law of disorder is here to stay.

Big bang cosmology violates fundamental scientific principles.

Big bang theory contradicts the Second Law because it requires the universe as a whole to order itself over time. Now, the Second Law does allow order to increase in one area as long as another area becomes more random. But since there are no areas outside the universe (by definition), the cosmos must become less and less ordered over time.[5] To believe otherwise is much like the expectation that dropping a nuclear bomb on a mountain will yield neat piles of earth rather than utter destruction. What we see in the universe is directly opposite to the expectation of evolutionary cosmologists. We observe a decaying universe whose overall order is in decline. Evolution cosmology directly defies this great law of science.

3. What was before the Big Bang?

While some say that matter and energy are eternal and were always present, the question remains: Where did everything come from? It had to come from an outside source. How did it begin? Again, the answer is that an outside source initiated it. Everything observed has a beginning and an end. Matter and energy are no exceptions. The beginning came from an outside source: God.

4. Is expansion of the universe observable?

Red shifts—the movement of light coming from objects in space to the red end of the spectrum—are regarded as evidence for the expansion of the universe. However, there are some 50 models for the process of expansion. There is confusion and little consensus on this issue. That is not surprising. After all, one is dealing with a gigantic universe from a limited frame of reference.

There are no clear answers at this time, just creative speculation. This is illustrated by cosmology's concept for the beginning—what has been termed the 'cosmic egg'. Never observed, the cosmic egg idea for the origin of the universe takes the universe backwards in time and shrinks all matter down many billions of times smaller than a single proton. The idea that all matter and energy could be collected in one place staggers the imagination and, of course, has no empirical foundation. Yet, there are mathematical models that depict the precise fraction of a second when this took place. This is presented as scientific fact and needs to be challenged.

"In the beginning God"

Big bang cosmology defies the Word of God. Genesis 1:1 and Hebrews 11:3 together indicate that God created all the components of the universe from nothing. We know that the God who created the universe is the sum total of rationality and logic. The Big bang, however, denies rationality and long-held scientific principles. It does demonstrate that evolution is based on an amazingly credulous faith. The facts do not support these far-reaching claims.

All heavenly bodies came into being on the fourth day of creation, according to the Genesis account. The Hebrew word for lights, *maor*, means luminous lights. It was on the fourth day that the nuclear furnaces of stars began to burn, producing heat and radiating the whole universe. The first light was not from the stars; it was from God. On the first day God spoke, "'Let there be light,' and there was light." (Genesis 1:3).

Light is part of the electromagnetic spectrum, which includes gamma rays, x-rays, ultraviolet, infrared, microwave, and radio waves. When the first light came into the universe, it was accompanied with these other forms. The Creator, Jesus Christ, who spoke light into existence, would later, as he walked on earth, relate light to eternal life. He said, "I am the light of the world. Whoever follows me will not walk in darkness, but will have the light of life" (John 8:12).

The billions upon billions of stars in the cosmos are a majestic display. What is the purpose of all those stars and heavenly bodies? The Scripture points out very clearly that the purpose for the creation of the stars on the fourth day was to be "for signs and for seasons, and for days and years" (Genesis 1:14). A great astronomical clock that never fails was formed by God in the heavens for us to keep order and have dominion over God's creation.

Not only do we have a timepiece to mark seasons, days, and years, but as God stated, we have 'a sign' to remind us of his everlasting presence—one marked in a heavenly realm that appears endless in size and space. The cosmos is filled with the evidence of God's glory and sovereignty. It is a sign to man to remind him of his position in time and space as he probes the heavens with sophisticated telescopes. We are simply brought to our knees knowing that there is one far greater than us who created the magnificent universe. Big bang cosmology is not science, but a belief that attempts to deny to the Creator proper recognition for His most magnificent signs in the universe.

> Lift up your eyes on high and see: who created these? He who brings out their host by number, calling them all by name, by the greatness of his might, and because he is strong in power not one is missing.
>
> —Isaiah 40:26

Notes

1. Nancy R. Pearcey and Charles B. Thaxton, *The Soul of Science*, Crossway Books, Wheaton, Illinois, 1994, p. 91.
2. Douglas F. Kelly, *Creation and Change*, Mentor: Ross-Shire, Great Britain, 1997.
3. David Cline, "The Search for Dark Matter," *Scientific American*, Vol. 288, March 2003, p. 52.
4. Abraham Loeb, as cited by Marcus Chown, Let there be Light, *New Scientist*, Vol. 157, February 7, 1998, p. 30.
5. Carl Wieland, *World Winding Down: Understanding the 'Law of Disorder'—And how it demands a Creator*, Creation Book Publishers, Powder Springs, Georgia, 2012.

Chapter Three

Evidence from the Earth

How the earth (and other planets) began is still an open question in evolutionary circles. Evolutionists tend to agree that the earth was formed about 4.6 billion years ago, starting from a very hot, gaseous state and eventually cooling down.

Creationists maintain that the earth began with the Creator, who miraculously formed the crust of the earth on the third day by separating the land from the water, as is stated in Genesis:

> And God said, "Let the waters under the heavens be gathered together into one place, and let the dry land appear." And it was so. God called the dry land Earth, and the waters that were gathered together he called Seas. And God saw that it was good.
>
> —Genesis 1:9–10

Evolutionists criticize creationists for what they consider an unreasonable and unintelligent faith in the Word of God. The critics fail to recognize that the Word of God is the *Logos* (John 1:1), the 'intelligence' of the universe. Genesis 1:9–10 above demonstrates this. It emphasizes the separation of the land from the sea, which could also be understood as the separation of a solid landmass from a liquid water medium.

Chemists define the formation of crystals as a process in which the salts that are dissolved in liquid medium separate and form a solid crystal at set conditions. It is interesting to note that granite rock is made up of four different types of minerals, each with a unique crystalline structure.

One could logically propose, then, that as God separated the land from the water, massive foundational rock structures were formed. Nobody can be sure, because no one knows exactly the process God used. However, the proposition that God used this separation of solid from liquid makes better scientific sense than the evolutionists' hot gas.

Genesis explains the formation of the earth's crust more plausibly than evolution.

The process by which rocks and minerals are made—the separation of solid from water—can be observed today. Rock comes from the earth's magma, which is a molten fluid inside the earth. Magma is composed of various metals and oxygen compounds. Along with these compounds is locked-up water vapor under tremendous pressure and heat. For magma to become rock, it must cool by coming to the surface. The heat of the magma causes rock above it to melt, allowing the magma closer to the surface. The magma cools before breaking the top layer and forms a crystalline hard rock. Granite is a great example of this rock formation. Another way magma comes to the surface is by an exploding volcano. The magma, once it abruptly breaks the surface of the earth, is called 'lava'. It comes out of the volcano with a great amount of steam, and as it flows onto the surface of the earth, it begins to cool and eventually hardens. 'Obsidian' is an example of rock formed from lava.

It is important to note that locked-up water vapor had an important role in making crystalline rock. The minerals that were formed went through a complicated process, combining and recombining, to form a stable chemical structure. As the minerals cooled, the separation of water from solid continued, until different kinds of minerals mixed, forming the rocks we observe today. It is obvious in the formation of a basic rock type that there is separation of water and solid. This is an observed scientific fact.

When we look at the earth's crust—this massive exterior shell—we can only marvel at the creative force that made it. Is this the result of random elemental collisions, which over millions of years formed the rocks we see today? Or, is this evidence of the workmanship of an intelligent designer? Did God purposely leave us a model of rock formation in the magma and lava of the earth that would lead to His Word? Is the principle of separation of solid from water, or 'land' from the 'seas', a more intelligent alternative than what we are being taught today? The evidence speaks loudly and clearly and points to a Creator God.

What do the rocks tell us about the Flood?

Rocks contain important evidence about the origin of the earth. Geologists classify rocks into three basic types, based upon the processes by which the rocks are formed. The first type is igneous rock, which is formed from magma. If magma reaches the earth's surface, it changes into the lava that spills from volcanoes. Once the rocks hit the surface, they are subject to environmental factors such as wind, rain, and even catastrophic events (like a worldwide Flood). These factors will cause rock to fracture into small pieces that become cemented together. Cement is made up of chemicals that, when mixed with water, harden in a short period of time. Rocks that are made up of small fractures or sediments are classified as sedimentary. The third type of rock is metamorphic—rock that has changed dramatically into a new chemical composition. For instance, limestone changes into marble when placed under tremendous heat and pressure.

> The rocks contain evidence of a worldwide deluge.

A set of basic questions arises when one considers the processes required to form these three kinds of rock. The answers offered by the evolutionary model leave gaping holes in the search for intelligent conclusions. The catastrophic worldwide Flood model offers a more rational, coherent framework for answering these basic questions.

1. How do the sedimentary rocks get hard?

Sedimentary rock needs water for cementing the tiny particles of sediment together. Where did the water come from? Evolutionists resolve this dilemma by waving the magic wand of 'time'. They insist that the sediments are washed into rivers, lakes, and oceans, and then fall to the bottom and pile up in layers. After many years, these sediments harden in layers, with those on the bottom hardening first. The problem with this theory is that there are beds of sedimentary rock everywhere on top of the earth's crust. Most of the large mountain chains are made of sedimentary rocks. How did all those sediments collect and become cemented together to make towering mountains? The logical answer is a worldwide Flood.

2. Is there an alternative to time as the mechanism of rock formation?

Yes! Rock formation can be explained by means of two processes, compaction and cementation, both of which could have occurred within one year after the waters of the Flood began to subside.

Global floodwater would have collected a huge amount of sediment. When the floodwater came to rest, the sediment would have begun to fall out. At the beginning, before the water started to evaporate, there would have been a great deal of pressure on the bottom layers. This would cause compaction. Creation geologist John Morris explains this as a 'pancake effect'.

> When a pancake layer of sediments is covered with other pancakes, the sand grains are pushed closer together; squeezing the water out. Compaction is the first step in turning sediment into a sedimentary rock, but not the only step.[1]

The second step is cementation. The glue that hardens the rock is generated by the warm water and minerals produced by the effects of the Flood. It does not take a long time for the rock to harden into layers. The layers that are observed are actually strata of sediments called, as John Morris put it, "pancakes".

This process need not take a long time. Remember, making sedimentary rocks is like preparing cement. To make cement, you need to have the proper ingredients and the right conditions. The waters would have been warm and deep at one time, giving the added energy needed for compaction. The worldwide Flood model provides the massive amount of water and sediment that would be needed to build the thick 'pancake' layering for the mountains present today. It makes for a more intelligent alternative.

3. What supplied the massive pressure and heat needed to make metamorphic rocks?

The heat and pressure required to make the vast amount of metamorphic rock in the earth's crust is not available today. The source of energy to do that has to be tremendous and is not presently observed anywhere on earth. A catastrophic

Flood that is spoken of in Genesis 6–9 could produce the forces needed to create metamorphic rock on the scale we now observe.

4. Why are fossils found in abundance on every continent?

Fossils are traces of plant and animal life that existed in the past and are found only in sedimentary rocks. Creationists believe that fossils were deposited during the global Flood, an obvious source of the water needed for both compaction and cementation. Fossils number in the trillions and suggest a swift, catastrophic event that buried them before any decay or decomposition occurred.

Rocks at one time had to be soft or have a liquid flow over them and bury them. Castings of thousands of fish have been found in sedimentary layers. If these fish had lain on the ground exposed to the elements, they would have disintegrated rapidly. Fish bones and scales do not harden … they scatter. Yet there are fossilized castings that show bone, and even scale, as if somebody took a picture and embedded it in the rocks. One would have to conclude that these fossils, as observed today, had to be the result of a catastrophic event that would cause rapid burial. The fossil evidence points to a worldwide Flood.

Fish fossil

Geological column and inherent problems

The geological column is a popular timetable used to date different strata by the use of fossils. Geologists have found that classifying rocks by comparison of fossils in all parts of the world is a very valuable tool. Part of the historical geological record is made using index fossils that span 570 million years. Theoretically, the whole geological record goes back in time some two billion years. These index fossils have specific characteristics. Most come from marine hard shell material. Of all the millions and millions of fossils, 95 percent are marine in nature. Index fossils have to fit certain criteria. They must:

1. Be found over wide areas
2. Be unique and distinguishable in character

3. Be of an organism that lived for a short period of time
4. Be present in abundance in rock layers.

Fossils, in general, are distributed by kind, as follows:
• 95% shallow water invertebrates, mostly shellfish
• 4.75% algae and plants
• 0.238% insects and remaining invertebrates
• 0.013% fish, amphibians, reptiles, birds and mammals[2]

A tidy sequence?

The geological column theorizes that the complexity of fossils in the ground will increase as one ascends the column toward the earth's surface. If you were to dig a big hole, you might expect to find, according to the geological column, an orderly progression of fossils, with the most simple at the bottom and the more complex toward the top. The theory holds that successive strata are marked with index fossils. It is important to note that sedimentary rocks, the rocks in which all fossils are found, cannot be dated directly by radioisotope dating methods; instead, these rocks are often dated by means of index fossils.

Ammonite fossil

Were you to find an index fossil, you would be able to determine its age by locating it in a diagram of the geological column, and seeing what age has been assigned to that rock layer. But how were the ages of the layers and their index fossils originally determined? Their ages were assigned based on the presupposition that rock layers were deposited slowly and gradually, and that the fossil record represents a succession of life forms over millions of years. Of course, the evolutionists argue that this sequence of fossils is a record of evolution.

However, while it is true that there is a general order to the fossil record, the textbook depictions of the geological column present too tidy a picture. In fact, many fossils are out of sequence according to evolutionary expectations, like the footprints of four-legged land animals which appear 18 millions years earlier than *Tiktaalik*, the fish that evolutionists claim is just beginning to evolve legs.[3] Also, some organisms like the Wollemi pine tree disappear from the fossil record for spans allegedly representing millions of years, even though they are still alive today.[4]

Grand Canyon layers

It is common for scientists to discover fossilized creatures in rocks they previously thought were too old or too young to contain them.

Besides, nowhere in the earth is the complete geological column observable. There are only sections available in different parts of the world. One of the most impressive formations is the Grand Canyon. There are several geological layers representing the Paleozoic Era exposed in the canyon. Even with the biggest hole on earth, the Grand Canyon, the geological formations, compared to the complete record, are terribly incomplete.

The extensive research of John Woodmorappe, who has analyzed data from around the world on the geological column, has led him to the following conclusion:

> Since only a small percentage of the earth's surface obeys even a significant portion of the geological column, it becomes an overall exercise of gargantuan special pleading and imagination for the evolutionary-uniformitarian paradigm to maintain that there ever were geological periods. The claim of their having taken place to form a continuum of rock/life/time of ten biochronologic 'onion skins' (geological column) over the earth is therefore a fantastic and imaginative contrivance.[5]

More geological challenges

The geological column concept also relies on the presupposition that long periods of time elapsed between each stratum. John Morris, a geologist and the President of the Institute for Creation Research, notes evidence in his book, *The Young Earth*, that contradicts this claim and points to the rapid deposition of rock material by a catastrophic event.

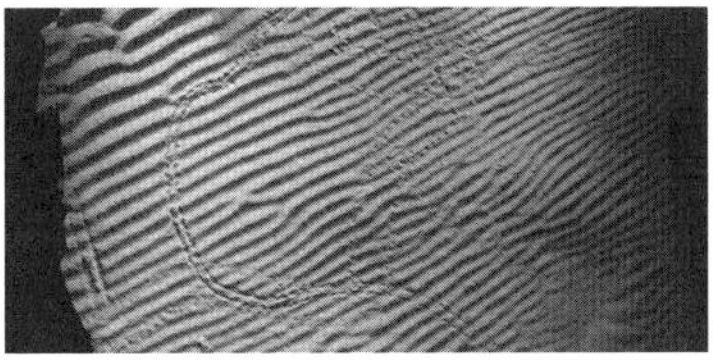

Ripple fossil

1. Surface features

Ripple marks, raindrops and animal tracks

are found on sedimentary rocks. These imprints had to have the right conditions to harden. The rock material was apparently soft enough to make impressions, but had the capacity to harden quickly.

2. Bioturbation

Biological activity on the top of the surface can easily destroy the internal structure of sedimentary rock layering. The earth has always been biologically active, and therefore all the layering effects should be void. This is not the case. There is a distinct pancake layering in the geological record, demonstrating that little or no biological activity has been going on. The layering had to take place catastrophically.

3. Lack of soil layer

If each layer represents a long period of time, then activity on the earth by living and nonliving forces would have produced weathering, water erosion, and chemical deterioration. Biological interactions with earth would have formed a soil layer. Soil supports all living systems. The layers of rocks have no fossilized evidence of a past existence of organic soil. There is layer upon layer of rock and no hard evidence of unambiguous ancient soil horizons. One would have to conclude that layering of this rock was a one-time event, not multiple periods of time ranging in the millions of years, as evolutionists propose for the geological column.

4. Soft sediment deformation

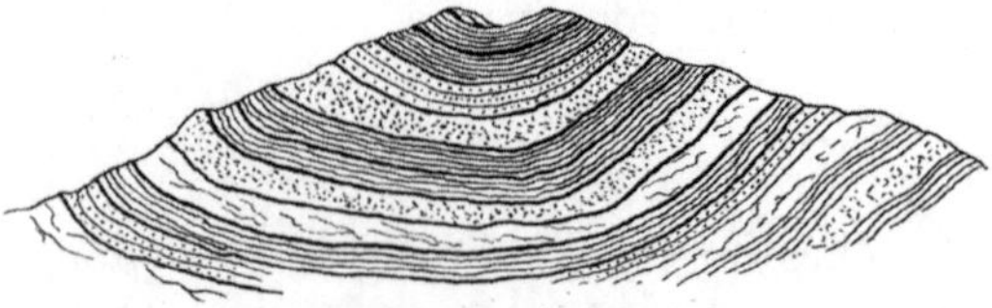

Bent rock layers

The sedimentary layers are deformed in places. These layers bend like a wave or contort in a downward or upward fashion. How does hard, brittle rock bend without cracking? According to the worldwide Flood model, there were heat and sediments falling out during the Flood, giving a layering effect. The sediments were soft and could be molded easily at the beginning of this process. They gradually settled and hardened in the way we see them today.

5. Polystrate fossils

Numerous examples of trees that have been petrified and pass through several layers of rocks have been discovered in the fossil record. These stone trees are embedded vertically in the layers of the geological column, supposedly across thousands or millions of years. This is bad news for evolutionists. Creationists have explained this scientifically, using the Flood model, demonstrating that the catastrophic force of floodwaters and movement of the surface of the earth dislodged these trees. As the sediments began to fall, making layers of rock, so did the weighted, unbalanced trees. They landed vertically in the sediments. When the earth began to drain, the sedimentary rocks were hardened in layers, surrounding the tree and making it a geological phenomenon.

Fossils and evolution

In theory, the fossil record ought to be an excellent source of evidence for evolution. Given the claim that it is the record of hundreds of millions of years of evolutionary change, it should show examples of the development of each species at every stage of the evolutionary process. In fact, it does not. It is an embarrassment. Over the decades, paleontologists have admitted that the fossil record is woefully incomplete from an evolutionary perspective.

> The fossil record does not support evolution, but the idea in Genesis that God created distict and separate kinds of organisms.

The evolution tree that is proposed should be supported with actual fossil evidence. When we evaluate what has been found, one would have to conclude that the cupboard is bare. Millions upon millions of fossils have been collected to date, but comparatively few fossils are even put forward as transitional forms, that is, fossils of organisms in an intermediate stage of development between steps on the evolutionary ladder. Furthermore, these fossils are often fragmentary and open to many interpretations. Their intermediate status is based on highly questionable claims, often disputed by other evolutionary scientists.

In actuality, the fossil record supports the idea of distinct and separate kinds, just as is spoken of in Genesis 1:24: "And God said, 'Let the earth bring forth living creatures according to their kinds …'".

Dr. Tom Kemp, curator of the zoological collection at the Oxford Museum of Natural History, wrote:

As is now well known, most fossil species appear instantaneously in the record, persist for some millions of years virtually unchanged, only to disappear abruptly.[6]

The late Stephen Jay Gould, a Harvard paleontologist, said:

The evolutionary trees that adorn our textbooks have data only at the tips and nodes of their branches; the rest is inference, however reasonable, not the evidence of the fossils.

The extreme rarity of transitional forms in the fossil record persists as the trade secret of paleontology—we fancy ourselves as the only true students of life's history, yet to preserve our favoured account of evolution by natural selection, we view our data as so bad that we never see the very process we profess to study.

The history of most fossil species include two features particularly inconsistent with gradualism: 1) Stasis—most species exhibit no directional change during their tenure on earth. They appear in the fossil record looking much the same as when they disappear; morphological change is usually limited and directionless; 2) Sudden appearance—in any local area, a species does not arise gradually by the steady transformation of its ancestors; it appears all at once and 'fully formed'.[7]

Notes

1. John Morris, *The Geology Book*, Master Books, Green Forrest, Arkansas, 2000, p. 36.
2. John Morris, *The Young Earth: Revised and Expanded*, Master Books, Green Forest, Arkansas, 2007, p. 74.
3. Tas Walker, Is the famous fish-fossil finished? *Tiktaalik*, the transitional star, faces an evolutionary dead-end, *Creation* **32**(3):38–39, July 2010.
4. Sensational Australian tree… like 'finding a live dinosaur', *Creation* **17**(2):13, March 1995.
5. John Woodmorappe, *Studies in Flood Geology*, Institute for Creation Research, El Cajon, California, 1999, p. 128.

6. Tom Kemp, A Fresh Look at the Fossil Record, *New Scientist*, Vol. 108, Dec. 5, 1985, p. 67.

7. Stephen Jay Gould, Evolution's Erratic Pace, *Natural History*, May 1977, pp. 13–14.

Chapter Four

Evidence from Life

Darwin recognized that the fossil record, as it existed, had serious problems. He admitted that the record, as it stood then, offered an argument against evolution. It was Darwin's hope that continued fossil exploration would reveal more evidence demonstrating an unbroken succession of life forms from simple to complex.

During Darwin's lifetime, a rich repository of some of the oldest fossils ever discovered was found in Cambria (the classical name for Wales). It is called the 'Cambrian Explosion'. Because of its place in the geological column, only the simplest life forms should have been found in the Cambrian layer. According to the theory, rock in this layer should contain fossils that would give us insight into the very first stages of evolution. Surprise! What was found was totally unexpected! Paleontologists discovered what they call 'bursts' of life forms that appear abruptly, representing the major groups of animals with their radically different body plans. It confounded evolutionary thinking, because greatest distinctions between life forms appeared first, before the smaller variations.

These fossils were said to date back to what came to be called the Cambrian period—making them 485 to 542 million years old. Rocks assigned to the Cambrian have also been found in Utah, Canada, Siberia, Greenland, and China. During the time of Darwin (in the mid 1800s) the rock layer below the Cambrian stratum was believed to be older yet and was devoid of fossils, because it was believed that the heat and pressure from above had destroyed any traces of life. This pre-Cambrian section comprises most, some 88 percent, of the geological column.

More recently, an effort has been made to divide the pre-Cambrian rock into other geological layers. The Ediacaran Period allegedly precedes the Cambrian in time and is 542–635 million years old—a period in which fossilized soft body organisms or extinct worm-like creatures were found. There is uncertainty as to what fossils belong in the Ediacaran. Some that may belong in the Ediacaran are simply blobs. The Ediacaran Period is contained within the Proterozoic Eon, which evolutionists have assigned to be between 542 million and 2.5 billion years old. Fossils found in the Proterozoic are microscopic organisms including bacteria, fungi, protists (amoeba, paramecium, algae) and others. The fossils found in this eon are very much like what we see today and can be found on any other layer.

> The simplest life forms in the fossil record are still extremely complex, contradicting the evolutionary model.

Cambrian fossils are of every basic body type. It is because they are so numerous and appear so abruptly in the geological record that this find has been called the Cambrian Explosion. Organisms from hard-shelled clams to mollusks to extinct trilobites, and even fish, have been discovered in this layer. This vast array of organisms, all found on one layer, is a huge problem to the evolutionary thesis that slow change over eons accounts for all life forms now in existence.

The big problem

Fully-formed fossils, representing so many kinds of animals without any ancestral forms, present a tremendous problem to evolution. Darwin's theory states that all life forms evolved from simple to complex, from molecule to man. But in the Cambrian layer, where one would expect to find fossil evidence of lower forms—organisms in an earlier stage of evolution—none have been found. Even if one goes down further to the next layers, in the Proterozoic, no fossils that show any connection to the organisms found in the Cambrian appear. Again, the Cambrian explosion can not be explained by evolution, while creationists interpret this layer as the fossil record of those creatures that lived on the bottom of the ocean at the time of the Flood.

The amazing trilobite

Trilobites are extinct soft body animals that once moved along the bottom of the sea and had features similar to a horseshoe crab. They typically vary in size from 3–10 cm (1.2–3.9 inches) and have a ridged shell divided by three distinct lobes, the feature for which they are named. A few trilobite fossils have been found that measure 72 cm (2.4 feet). These creatures are found in the Cambrian layer, accompanied by many different kinds of creatures. Evolutionists get excited about old-age fossils, particularly the trilobite, because it is found in the Cambrian layer and thought to be some 500 millions years old. One would assume from evolutionary theory that the trilobite, given its putative age and place in the geological column, would be simple in form. Not so.

Trilobite fossils

Like any other living system, trilobites have inherent complexity. One of the most revealing examples of complexity found in trilobites is their aggregate eye, a feature found in some, though not all trilobites. This very unique eye features an upper lens, which is hardened calcite, and a lower lens designed to correct the ray pattern to a focal point. It has rods in slightly different positions, similar to an insects' compound eye. The aggregate eye is also called schizochroal and is one of the finest optical systems designed.

> The design of the schizochroal eye makes it unique among eyes; perhaps even to the point of being the best optical system known in the biological world. This design, in fact seems to far exceed the needs of the trilobite. The origin of the design of the schizochroal eye is not understood by means of any known natural cause. Rather, it is understood as being due to an intelligent (design-creating) cause, through a process involving remarkably high manipulative ability. Among available hypotheses, creation of God is the most reasonable hypothesis for the origin of the complexity of the trilobite's schizochroal.[1]

The fossil record's real testimony

Randomness

The evolutionary hypothesis holds that simple organisms will change into more complicated forms slowly through time. For that reason, evolutionists divide the fossil record into theoretical periods, such as the Cambrian and Ediacaran, in order to show from the fossil record the progress of life up the evolutionary scale. It is not working out that way. As more and more fossils are discovered, these theoretical divisions are disappearing. Fossils keep appearing at the wrong places, suggesting that the system needs to change. As fossils are discovered, it is apparent that the organisms are not simple and that they challenge, by their unexpected complexity, evolutionary assumptions about the fossil record.

Living fossils

Living fossils are fossils of plants and animals that are not extinct, but still exist today. For example, more than 84 percent of insects still in existence have been found in the fossil record as far back as what evolutionists tell us was 100 million years ago. Other living fossils include the following:

- The Chambered Nautilus
  "It remains essentially the same as its ancestors of 180 million years ago . . . a living link with the past." *National Geographic*, January 1976
- The Praying Mantis, fossilized in amber, is dated to 40 million years ago
- The Coelacanth, thought to have become extinct 70 million years ago, but was found alive in the 1930s off the coast of Madagascar.

Even more complex than you think

Michael Behe, an outspoken biochemist, is challenging the foundations on which biological evolution rests. With the publication of *Darwin's Black Box* in 1996, he presented an academic challenge to traditional Darwinian thought. As a biochemist, he began to question how small microorganisms could evolve from raw components. Although he is not a biblical creationist, he came to the conclusion that, given the fine details of these living systems, they could not have come from any known natural processes. This led him to the only alternative answer: an outside Intelligent Designer.

Biochemistry explains how all the component parts of a living system work together and how the molecules act together. The light microscope, pushed to its limits, could reach down to one-tenth the size of a bacteria cell. Many of the substructures could not be visualized completely, and many were still hidden. In the 1950s, with the aid of the new electron microscope, cell structure took on a new meaning. The electron microscope has the capacity, with the aid of an electron beam, to magnify an object 500,000 times.

> Living organisms have extremely complex, integrated systems that can only come from an intelligent Creator.

With the capacity to view the cell in such incredible detail, many new subcellular structures were discovered. Behe, in his book, reflects on the fact that each of these substructures have their own set of biochemical instructions. Such detail exponentially increased the complexity of the cell. A hundred years after Darwin, the simple cell suddenly became immensely complicated, with countless systems all entwined with each other to contribute to the total biological purpose of sustaining life.

Molecular machines

The molecular machines of the cell are the proteins. These molecular protein machines are the basic material of which cells are made. They provide structure and chemically interact with other molecules and particles of the cell. Proteins are composed of 100 or more amino acid units strung together in different sequences to make a long chain. An amino acid chain needs help from a molecular machine called a chaperonin so that it can properly fold into the three dimensional shape of a protein. These folded proteins have their own complexity and are useful for specific cell functions, as in building structures or chemically reacting with other molecules.

It is in the details that evolution fails so miserably. The molecular structures from which proteins are made have always been challenging. Today they continue to give biochemists new revelations of how living systems work. These proteins make up the different structures of the cell, which include the nucleus, mitochondrion, ribosome, cell membrane, vacuole and many others.

Cells are mobile and move with the help of different protein structures. Bacterial cells move in a variety of ways. A moving tail, called a flagellum, propels one type of bacteria cell. This tail is made of hundreds of different types of proteins that function just like a rotary propeller moving at impressive speed. Behe suggests that the flagellum paddling mechanism is made of three substructures: the paddle, a rotor, and a motor. The bacterial flagellum is a marvelously designed substructure with the following unique characteristics:

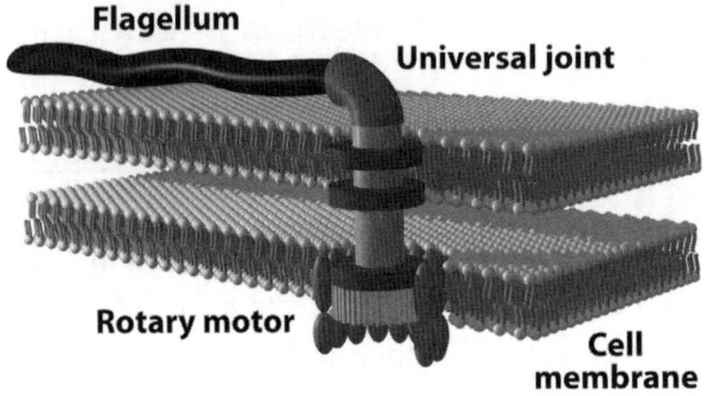

- Tail moves at 100,000 rpm
- Moves in two directions: forward and reverse
- Reversing after ¼ of a turn
- Acid (proton) driven
- At least 40 operational parts
- Rotary motor cooled by water

Irreducible complexity

Behe introduced the concept of 'irreducible complexity' to describe what he found in the myriad micro systems all functioning together within a cell. He found component parts as simple as a molecule synchronized with other molecules, like the mechanical gears of an expensive Swiss watch. Just as the watch would stop if one of the gears failed—if a molecule were altered in a biologically elaborate system—the organism could die. In the words of Behe:

> By irreducibly complex, I mean a single system composed of several well-matched, interacting parts that contribute to the basic function, wherein the removal of any one of the parts causes the system to effectively cease functioning.[2]

This principle of irreducible complexity can be seen at every level of biological function—from molecules to cells to organs to organisms. The simple tail of a one-cell bacteria, as described above, has at least 40 moving parts. If one of those parts failed to function, the tail would cease to work. Without the tail, the cell could not move; and without movement, the cell would die for lack of nutrients.

No room for evolution

Irreducible complexity makes a powerful argument for design. For a system to function, not only are all parts needed, but a set of instructions are needed as well for how the parts should work together. To assemble a new lawn mower out of the box, not only do you need all the parts, you need an instruction manual (hopefully, with lots of pictures) to put it together. Cell assembly is a far more complex task than putting together a lawn mower. The parts and instructional manual for the cell did not produce themselves. They had to come from a divine planner, the Creator—Jesus Christ.

The study of biochemistry demonstrates how the basic materials in a cell or other living system function together. This academic discipline majors on the details of life and is usually taught in the upper level of undergraduate or the graduate level at colleges and universities. It is interesting to note that evolution has no place in this discipline. Many biochemistry texts completely ignore evolution. When mentioned, it is usually in passing. By its nature, biochemistry deals with measurable, empirical data. It seeks out the order and design in living systems, a process that, if one is open-minded, leads to the deduction that there is an intelligent Creator. This, after all, was Behe's final conclusion:

> The simplicity that was once expected to be the foundation of life has proven to be a phantom; instead, systems of horrendous, irreducible complexity inhabit the cell. The resulting realization that life was designed by intelligence is a shock to us in the twentieth century who have gotten used to thinking of life as the result of simple natural laws.[3]

DNA from a Higher Source

It was front-page news nationwide. "Genetic Code of Human Life Is Cracked by Scientists," the *New York Times* announced on June 27, 2000. This marked the first time the whole human DNA code—the blueprint of life—had been mapped. This enormous project, formally called the Human Genome Project, involved hundreds of scientists in a multibillion-dollar experiment funded by medical research grants from several countries. They found the exact sequencing of 3.2 billion chemical building blocks (abbreviated with the letters A, T, C, and G) in the DNA of a human. All sorts of wonderful benefits were predicted with

> The molecular information in DNA had to come from an outside source of higher intelligence.

this discovery, including a cure for cancer.

Unfortunately, the press reacted too quickly. Now it appears that there is a long road ahead, with many difficult hurdles to clear. What was really uncovered was similar to four letters strung out in a sequence of 3.2 billion base pairs. Much work still has to be done to understand the meaning of those letters. The term 'cracking the genetic code' implies that scientists understand what the code means. The mapping of all that human genetic information is a great accomplishment. But to say that it is understood? This is nothing but a puffed-up exaggeration by the press.

Evolutionary scientists once concluded that out of the billions of bits of DNA base pair data, only 5 percent are actually used. Beyond that extremely small percentage, the rest was labeled as 'junk' DNA, or evolutionary 'leftovers'. This so-called 'junk' DNA is something we don't fully understand at the present time, but as research continues, new insights are being revealed as to its genetic function. Creationists argue that junk DNA performs important regulatory functions, and could have been used to enable a rapid post-Flood biological adjustment.

Presently, there are still large gaps of knowledge that remain. To illustrate this even further, the geneticists have recently found that genes can have more than one function. For instance, the Distal-less gene develops the appendages of mice, sea urchins, spiny worms and velvet worms. The same gene produces different structures. This phenomenon is being intensely studied and is still a big mystery. Clearly, the genetic code is extremely complicated.

What does DNA look like?

James Watson, an American biologist, and Francis Crick, a British physicist at Cambridge, England, worked out the structure of DNA in 1953. DNA is the foundational information storage system of life. Finally, the mysterious chemical structure that controls every living organism was revealed to all mankind. All life is controlled by a simple double helix structure. This is like a nanoscale spiral staircase, where the stairs are made by four chemical bases: Guanine (G), Cytosine

(C), Adenine (A), and Thymine (T). The 'stairs' connect two strands comprising alternating deoxyribose (a type of sugar) and phosphate. This explains the name of DNA: deoxyribonucleic acid.

The DNA molecule is a very long, microscopically thin string that is tightly bound together. When it unravels, it unzips the double helix, and the two segments open up, exposing a sequence of the four base pairs listed above. Since the molecule is very long, the sequence of base pairs on each side carries an immense amount of information. When both sides of the DNA molecule open, the four base codes send instructions from the nucleus of the cell to build proteins. The simplicity of two base pairs is amazing—being sequenced over a long molecule and having the potential to contain the information from which all life is derived.

Amazing properties

DNA has extraordinary properties, including the following:

- DNA is a very thin filament measuring 0.000,000,002 meters thick in diameter.
- DNA is so thin that a strand of DNA long enough to reach the sun would weigh only half a gram.
- The DNA in each human cell would be about 2 m (6 feet) long if totally unraveled.
- If an adult human's entire DNA were to be unwound, it would extend 184 billion kilometers. That is an unimaginably long molecular string that would go to the sun and back, a distance of 310 million kilometers (or 186 million miles), some 596 times.
- DNA weighing an amount equivalent to 1/15 of a postage stamp contains all the DNA needed to make 5 billion people.
- The information in the DNA of each human cell would fill 850 Bible-sized books.

How is the information stored?

Information is derived from the order in which the four bases, or chemical 'letters' appear. But this order is meaningless unless decoded by many decoding machines, including the *ribosome*. This is a real chicken-and-egg problem: the instructions to build these decoding machines are in the DNA, but these instructions can't be decoded without already-existing decoding machines.

The code produces genetic information for proteins to do their work, making cells to form a plant, frog, turtle, human or any living system. There are at least 50,000 different proteins in living systems. In DNA, the base pairs function in three groups. In threes, the information code is given to produce amino acids. The amino acids then bond together, usually in the thousands, to make the proteins essential for living systems.

The intelligence center of the cell is the *nucleus* where the DNA is found. The DNA molecule is considered the greatest information carrier known to man. The tiny DNA molecules are tightly wound up. For example, the E. coli chromosome has 300,000 twists in the space 1 mm. DNA's information density is a staggering 1.88×10^{21} bits per cm^3. The sum of all human knowledge in all books is 10^{18} bits. All the libraries of the world combined could never match the amount of information in one cubic centimeter, or 0.4 of a cubic inch, of DNA.

The sum total of knowledge currently stored in the libraries of the world is estimated at 10^{18} bits. If this information could be stored in the DNA molecules, one percent of the volume of a pinhead would be sufficient for this purpose. If, on the other hand, this information were stored with the aid of mega chips, we would need a pile higher than the distance between the earth and the moon.[4]

DNA: self-replication

Not only is DNA a magnificent information machine, it also has phenomenal replication accuracy. After all, its basic function is to transfer genetic information in order to continue living processes. Since cells make every living organism, it is of extreme importance that no information is lost in the duplication process. Cells, after they divide, must have identical genetic information without any transfer of mistakes. To replicate, the DNA molecule in a bacteria cell unravels at an amazing speed of 10,000 revolutions per minute.

The chemical structure of the bases provides the means for replicating the information—as a cell divides, and from parent to child. The letter A of one strand always matches a T of the other, and vice versa; and G always matches C. So the each DNA strand can be copied to make another strand which is analogous to a photographic negative. Here as well, there are complex machines needed for the copying, in particular *DNA polymerase.* This is another chicken-and-egg problem: the instructions to build DNA are also stored on DNA, but they can't be passed on to the next generation without pre-existing copying machines.

This replication is also very accurate, thanks to error-checking machines:

> The replication is so precise, that it can be compared to 280 clerks copying the entire Bible sequentially, each one from the previous one, with (at most) one single letter being transposed erroneously in the entire copying process.[5]

Once again, there is a chicken-and-egg problem: the instructions to build the error-checking machines are stored in the DNA. But without pre-existing error checking machines, these instructions would be degraded when the DNA is replicated. This would lead to worse error-checking machines, which would allow further degradation of the instructions, causing even worse machines. This would be an *error catastrophe*.

Only from an intelligent, outside source

The DNA code contains information that is translated into a program to make a specific protein. The protein is made to fulfill a biological need so the living system can function. There is a molecular transfer of information from the DNA molecule, which is programmed to be aware of the total needs of the whole living system. Biochemists have classified this marvelous process as 'the language of life'. It is apparent that the information system for all life is a wonder. The fact is that DNA is designed with such an ultimate excellence that it far surpasses what man has done and what he can do in the future. The amount of information stored and the way it is replicated is nothing but a miracle.

The code reveals a language that is in every gene. The complexity of this language, as mentioned above, far exceeds all human knowledge. It could not come from a material source. It is classified as a language not unlike a computer language. One would consider it ridiculous to assume that computer programming came from the computer chip. Every computer language was made from an outside source. Language uses a higher form of conceptual intelligence.

The late Dr. Wilder Smith demonstrated by a simple illustration the preposterous nature of the evolutionary idea that life came from inert matter. He compared the claim that life could be produced from inert matter to the idea of a blank book producing letters on its pages. In the case of the book, once all 26 letters are produced, they would then randomly combine to make words. These words would randomly mix to make sentences expressing complete thoughts. The random process would continue until a paragraph is formed. After that, paragraphs would randomly combine to make chapters and, finally, the same random process would produce the final product, the book. Not likely.

It is obvious that books are the product of an outside intelligence and that language is used to translate information. But evolution offers the irrational argument that the DNA code came from randomness. Dr. Smith's illustration makes it clear that the DNA code must originate from an outside intelligent source who has a plan and will use the letters to give us words or proteins. These proteins combine and form complete sentences—or cells. These cells combine and form paragraphs—or tissue. These tissues come together to form chapters—or organs. And the last step … these organs come together to form the book—or organism. All of these steps are programmed by an outside source, just as an author writes a book.

There is no man in the universe who could come up with this wonderful and awesome design for life. The evidence is clear. The complexity of any living system points to God. It is written in our genes that there is a God … so we are without excuse.

Statistically impossible!

As mentioned above, the protein molecule adds structure and function to every living cell. It is a long molecule that contains many subunit molecules all bonded together. These subunit molecules are called amino acids and are composed mainly of the elements nitrogen, oxygen, hydrogen, and carbon.

There are twenty kinds of amino acids involved in living plants and animals. A typical protein will have between 100 to 300 amino acids connected in a definite sequence. These amino acid sequences give the protein its shape and its potential to function as a basic unit of a component of the cell.

> It is statistically impossible for life to originate from non-life.

It should be noted that 19 out of the 20 types of biological amino acid molecules have a mirror image. Just as one's right hand is a mirror image of the left hand, so amino acids have a left- and a right-hand side to their molecular structure. If these amino acids were really formed in a primordial soup, as most evolutionists believe, they would be in a 50-50 (*racemic*) mixture. Amazingly, all observable living things are made of left-handed amino acids.

The protein is encoded with information based on the sequencing of its amino acids. Different sequences give different information which, in turn, allows the protein to perform various functions. This works because DNA operates with a several coded languages. The best known code operating on DNA is to make proteins: every three-letter sequence is called a *codon*, because it codes for one protein 'letter' or amino acid, or to start or stop the protein being made.

The sequencing of the amino acids begins in the DNA of the cell. Because DNA starts the process, it is very often called the information center of the cell. The big question is: Where does the DNA molecule receive its information? The answer is obvious—from an outside source—an intelligent Creator.

The improbable protein

A simple protein must have at least 100 amino acids bonded together in a set sequence. There are twenty amino acids to choose from, and, assuming they were available in number, the probability for the formation of a protein molecule would be impossible. The probability comes out to a staggering chance of one out of 10^{115}. That is 1 followed by 115 zeroes. This impossible-to-imagine number completely exceeds the statistical odds that it could ever happen. (Borel's Law holds that any probability less than 1 out of 10^{50} could not happen).

There is a 50 percent possibility that amino acids will be right- or left-handed. All protein molecules have left-handed amino acids. If a right-handed amino acid is added, it could be extremely toxic to the living system. With this new variable added to the above calculation for the statistical likelihood of the formation of a protein, one is confronted with an even greater problem. Given the criteria that not only do all 100 amino acids have a specific sequence, but they are all left-handed, the probability that this will occur works out to one in 10^{145}. This last calculation overwhelmingly demonstrates the massive problem evolution has in getting inert matter to form a protein. The statistical improbability for the next step, the formation of a single cell from all these improbable proteins, is beyond comprehension.

Seeking help in the heavens

When faced with these cold, hard statistics, what chance did evolution have? Francis Crick suggested life itself may be likened to a 'miracle'.

> An honest man, armed with all the knowledge available to us now, could only state that in some sense, the origin of life appears at the moment to be almost a miracle, so many are the conditions which would have had to have been satisfied to get it going.[6]

Thus some evolutionists looked heavenward for answers and came up with the idea of 'Directed Panspermia'. Crick helped popularize the hypothesis that some kind of extraterrestrial intelligence, aided by a UFO, carried life spores to the earth. Most evolutionists find this nothing but fantasy. In the real world, though, many do hope that an asteroid or trip to the planet Mars might reveal a life form that may have made it to earth untouched and ready to be incubated.

However, this is not only unscientific, it merely removes the very same problem to the untouchable reaches of the distant cosmos.

Kind after kind

Researchers have, by means of genetic breeding, changed a two-wing fruit fly into a four-wing fruit fly. The four-wing fruit fly consistently reproduces four-winged fruit flies. But although a new variety has been produced, it is not a new 'kind'. The mutant fruit fly is still a fruit fly. As a matter of fact, the four-winged fruit fly is a weakened form. The second set of wings do not help the fruit fly; they actually get in the way. Its ability to take flight is dangerously hindered. Having been selectively bred in the laboratory, this variant would not survive without the caring assistance of researchers. This is a poor example of evolution by mutation. The bottom line is that mutations always weaken an organism and never change it into something fundamentally different. The fruit fly remains a fruit fly.

> Changing one kind of living organism into another through 'beneficial mutations' is an improbable proposition.

Beneficial mutations?

Evolutionists often offer sickle cell anemia as an example of a beneficial mutation because those who have it have a reduced likelihood of getting malaria. Sickle cell anemia originates in a mutation in the hemoglobin molecule found in the red blood cells of our body. This mutation distorts the normal biconcave (concave on both sides) shape of the red blood cell. Presently, this disease affects millions of people worldwide; in the United States alone there are some 70,000 cases of active sickle cell anemia.

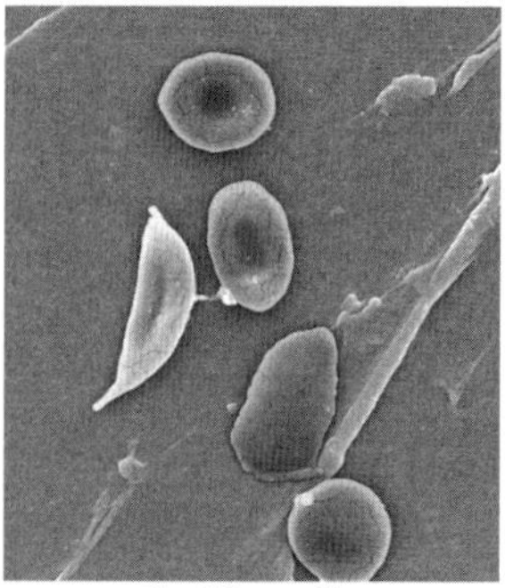

Sickle cells

OpenStax College - Anatomy & Physiology, Connexions Web site. cnx.org/content/col11496/1.6)

Sickle cell anemia is a hereditary blood disorder that is most common in people who trace their ancestry to Africa or India, regions where malaria outbreaks have taken many lives. However, those who have one sickle-cell gene and one healthy hemoglobin gene (i.e. are *heterozygous* in this trait) have minimal sickle-cell symptoms but also have malarial resistance. So since the mutant gene benefits its possessor, it is a beneficial mutation by definition. However, as will be shown, this is irrelevant for evolution.

Definitely a defect

Even this beneficial sickle cell mutation is most definitely a defect. There is no substitute for the optimal biconcave shape of normal hemoglobin molecules. This shape is tolerant to quick movement and designed perfectly for the effective transfer of oxygen to every cell in our body.

In the case of sickle cell anemia (SCA), the DNA that produces the proteins to make the hemoglobin in the red blood cells actually transfers one coding error. This error or genetic defect produces hemoglobin molecules that stick to each other when oxygen is released to the tissues. The defective hemoglobin molecules form long rigid chains that completely distort the shape of the red blood cell. Some of these distorted red blood cells actually form a distinct crescent shape and look like 'sickles'—hence the name 'sickle cell'.

These distorted red blood cells grow in size and can clog the capillaries, which limits the transfer of oxygen and causes severe pain to the extremities and throughout the body, including the chest cavity. It also leads to shortness of breath, infection, organ damage, and, in severe cases, can cause death. It also should be noted that sickle-shaped red blood cells die prematurely because of their large unstable shape. A normal red blood cell will last 120 days while a sickle cell can only survive 10 to 20 days. Patients with this disease often need blood transfusions to replace their lost hemoglobin.

However, a person who is heterozygous with the SCA gene usually doesn't have the misfolding that leads to the anemia. But when the malarial parasite (Plasmodium) invades one of his blood cells, it causes the hemoglobin to 'sickle' and deform the blood cell. The spleen detects this defective cell and destroys it along with the parasite.

It's important to note that this has nothing to do with evolution of more complex features. Rather, it is more akin to guerilla war against an invading army: guerillas might destroy a bridge on which the enemy is crossing. However, although it is 'beneficial' for the country to destroy the enemy, the country is poorer by one bridge. Similarly, the person destroys the malarial parasite but loses a blood cell in the process.

In any case, resistance to malaria at the cost of a dangerous blood disorder that leads to premature death does not confirm Darwin's idea that species evolve upward over time.[7]

Beneficial mutations "exceedingly rare"

Mutation statistics accumulated over several decades show that there is very little data to build a theory that evolutionary progress takes place by means of beneficial mutation. First, as shown, the usual examples of beneficial mutation are still destructive. Also, the late Motoo Kimura, a Japanese mathematical biologist, introduced in 1979 a statistical method for handling data on genetic mutations. He clearly demonstrated that most mutations are neutral in their effect. Very few are lethal and no beneficial mutations are represented in his graphical representation because the number is too small to be mathematically significant. According to J.C. Sanford, a geneticist from Cornell University who invented the 'gene gun', beneficial mutations "are exceedingly rare—much too rare for genome building."[8]

The development of bacterial resistance to antibiotics is often suggested by evolutionists as another proof for upward evolutionary progress through beneficial mutations. A careful molecular analysis shows quite the contrary. Mutant strains of bacteria that show resistance to antibiotic are hindered by a degradation of genetic information—meaning they have become less fit over time. "Clearly, the fitness of some mutant strains is permanently reduced (sometimes dramatically), and evolutionists have typically ignored such effects in their rush to promote antibiotic resistance as 'evolution in the Petri dish,'" according to microbiologist Dr. Kevin Anderson.[9] Just like SCA above, the resistance is caused by information-destroying mutations, even if they are beneficial.

Statistically insignificant

Dr. Jerry Bergman searched for the term 'beneficial mutations' in two biomedical journal databases containing 18.8 million records. While the term 'mutation' turned up 453,732 times, the phrase 'beneficial mutation' was used just 186 times, a statistically insignificant number (.041 percent) that agrees with Kimura's statistical analysis. As Bergman researched further he found that so-called 'beneficial mutations' always involved a loss of genetic information. He concluded: "Not a single clear example of an information growing mutation was located. It was concluded that molecular biology research shows that information-gaining mutations have not been documented."[10]

Perhaps the best way to summarize the overuse of the evolutionists' blind faith in 'beneficial mutations' is with Sanford's own words, "In conclusion, mutations appear to be overwhelmingly deleterious, and even when one may be classified as beneficial in some sense, it is still usually part of an over-all breakdown and erosion of information."[11]

No new information

A basic information principle must be violated for evolution to be true. For an organism to evolve upward from simple to complex, there must be an increase of genetic information. When mutations take place, however, there is an exchange of information or misinformation, but never an increase. The system is limited to what it has and, therefore, cannot create new information. Most frequently, information exchange leads to a *loss* of information. The loss of genetic information is consistent with the universal law of entropy.

It can be observed that errors in the genetic code are passed between generations. The rate of mutation is much too high to allow for evolution over millions of years. There are 100 to 300 misspellings of our genetic code passed on from one generation to the next. This might seem insignificant when we consider that the human genome contains 3 billions letters. However, the human race has six billion people, which means some 600 billion to 1.8 trillion genetic mistakes per generation.

Genetic load

If one includes other types of mutations, such as deletions, insertions, duplications, mitochondrial mutations and others, the number of individual mutations will be 1,000 times more for each person and for the whole population. As a result, our genetic endowment is being corrupted. This phenomenon of accumulating mutations is best termed as 'genetic load'.

According to Dr. Sanford, "The consensus among geneticists is that at present the human race is degenerating genetically, due to rapid mutation accumulation and relaxed natural selection pressure." The decline in our fitness as a species is thought to be taking place, Sanford writes, at the rate of one to two percent per generation.[12]

Such a great rate of decay in the genetic code does not fit with the six to seven million years it took for man to evolve according to the evolutionary model. It fits best with a biblical time frame of 6,000 years. This range of time was determined using a biological decay curve that was constructed using the rate of genomic degeneration.[13]

There is no time for evolution to take place with this type of genetic degeneration. The human race is subject to more variations of disease and sickness as the 'genetic load' increases. Man will have to work hard against the law of entropy to stay alive. Genetic deterioration certainly excludes the idea of upward evolutionary progress by which we move from tiny living molecules and organisms to man.

Chimp and human DNA

There has been a great deal of time, energy, and money invested for the purpose of developing advanced technology to investigate plant and animal DNA. The ability to isolate complete genetic alphabet sequences will no doubt start to give us a better understanding of the bio-molecular process. Evolutionists are at the door anxiously waiting to jump in and chant, "I told you that slow change of our genetic code is how we humans got here after all."

The October 9, 2006, cover of *Time* displayed a juvenile monkey's face just above the shoulder of an infant, with the provocative title, "How We Became

Human. Chimps and humans share almost 99 percent of their DNA. New discoveries reveal how we can be so alike—and yet so different."

Actually, the 99% genetic similarity claim is based on outdated and selective research. The true sequence similarity is unknown, but more recent studies have found dramatic differences that demolish the 1% myth.[14] But even if the difference was only one percent, would that mean men and monkeys are almost alike? Since there are 3 billion letters in our DNA, this would mean 30 million differences! As one writer for Smithsonian admits, "just a few percentage points translate into vast, unbridgeable gaps between species."[15]

No one will disagree after a visit to the zoo that chimps look more like us than any other animal. They rank high in intelligence and have a fairly complex social system in the animal kingdom, but there is a real difference between people and other primates. Physical similarities may exist, but the differences are so huge that we would never confuse an ape with a human. The proportions of the lengths of our arms and legs, the appearance of the neck, skull, pelvis, hands, and soft tissue structures—including our lips—clearly distinguish us from other species. Internally, our proteins are 71 percent different from that of a chimp. We have 46 chromosomes while a chimp has 48, and our Y chromosomes are radically different.[16]

More to it than the code itself

The most important point of comparison between genetic sequences is not how similar the genes are but how the genes act or are expressed. Even similar gene sequences may act very differently because of their interaction with other genes. Our physical appearance, for example, is controlled by just a few genes. The length and shape of our nose, eyebrows, complexion, eye and hair color, etc., are all modulated not by an army of genes but by the orders of a very few genes which work in dynamic harmony. Dramatic physical change does not necessarily have to be orchestrated by DNA directly.

Physical change without DNA difference

Giuseppe Sermonti, a distinguished geneticist from Italy, argues that it may not be DNA alone that determines the nature and structure of living things. There is a black box between DNA and the total function and purpose of an organism. Secular evolutionists who suppose that DNA changes can explain evolution need to heed Sermonti's eloquent warning: "My view is that the problem is rather how the organism makes use of DNA, getting it to work or keeping it silent, and how it selects its areas of interest. DNA is not the starting point."[17] Just because we find the complete genome does not mean that we understand how DNA functions. Sermonti says we have great mysteries still to explore in seeking to understand how DNA determines who we are.

Common designer, not common ancestor

Evolution holds that organisms with similar designs must descend from one common ancestor. This argument can be challenged by this question, "Does similarity mean we come from the same ancestry or does it mean we were created by the same designer?" That designer would be the master creator, who could produce an ultimate design for every niche in the physical and living universe. That creator would have to be the perfect designer who knows all things and therefore chose the ultimate design, a universal design that can be utilized with the greatest efficiency to maintain all life. The evidence points to one magnificent, intelligent Creator.

For example, you may notice that a car dealership has a wide selection of cars. Each car has four wheels, an internal combustion engine, steering wheel, and many other common features. Did you ever wonder if the common design would mean that there would be common descent? In other words, did the cars evolve themselves without any outside help? This, of course, is ridiculous, because we know that enormous diligence was needed to design each car model. Although their basic features are the same, they have many other unique qualities that make them attractive to potential buyers. Each car model began with a preplanned design and an outside intelligent creator.

Since there are ultimate designs that function for the exact purpose for which they were created, one may expect to witness repetitive patterns in the universe. The more repetitive a design, the closer it is to perfection. We observe in nature, for example, many animals that have appendages—such as legs or arms or digits.

Does similarity mean we come from the same ancestry? Evolution holds that all organisms have descended from one common ancestor. Creation holds that all living things come from one common source, and are created by one Creator who set out an ultimate design for the universe … and all that is in it.

> For by him all things were created… all things were created through him and for him.
> —Colossians 1:16

Notes

1. Kurt Wise, My Favorite Evidence for Creation, *Creation* **11**(4): 29, September 1989.
2. Michael Behe, *Darwin's Black Box*, The Free Press, New York, 1996, p. 39.
3. Behe, p. 252.
4. Werner Gitt, *Information, The Third Fundamental Quantity*, Lecture at 4th Europe Creationist Congress, 1990.
5. Werner Gitt, *In the Beginning Was Information*, CLV English Edition, Bielefeld, Germany, 1997, p. 90.
6. Francis Crick, *Life Itself: Its Origin and Nature*, Simon & Schuster, New York, 1981, p. 88.
7. Jonathan Sarfati, Exposing Evolution's Icon (interview with Felix Konotey-Ahulu), *Creation* **29**(1): 16–19, December 2006.
8. J.C. Sanford, *Genetic Entropy and the Mystery of the Genome*, Elim Publishing, Lima, New York, 2005, p. 27.
9. Kevin Anderson, Is Bacterial Resistance to Antibiotics an Appropriate Example of Evolutionary Change? *Creation Research Society Quarterly*, March 2005, Vol. 41, No. 4, pp. 318–326.
10. Jerry Bergman, Darwinism and the Deterioration of the Genome, *Creation Research Society Quarterly*, September 2005, Vol. 42, No. 2, pp. 104–114.
11. Sanford, p. 27.
12. Sanford, p. 45.
13. Sanford, p. 152.
14. Don Batten, The Myth of 1%: Human and chimp DNA are very different, *Creation* **36**(1): 35–37, January 2014.

15. R. Conniff, Monkey Wrench, *Smithsonian*, October 2001, pp. 102–104.
16. David Catchpoole, Y chromosome shock, *Creation* **33**(2): 56, April 2011.
17. Giuseppe Sermonti, *Why is a Fly Not a Horse*, Discovery Institute Press, Seattle, WA, 2005, p. 110.

Chapter Five

Evidence from Man

Darwin, in his *Descent of Man*, explained that his objective was to show that there is no fundamental difference between man and higher mammals. According to Darwin, there was a lineal descendant of all the organisms reaching up to man. He emphasized that there were no special creations from God along this lineage, but all were connected through gradual evolutionary change. Man was no exception.

Evolutionists have a compelling reason to demonstrate an evolutionary link between man and ape. They know that if they succeed, they will silence the arguments of those who believe in special creation. Without any question, evolution would triumph if the fossil evidence were to show the final evolutionary phase of an ape becoming man.

When it is announced that an ape-like fossil has been found, the news media lavishes uncritical ink and abundant space to the claims generated by the find. Time after time, however, when the original find of a supposed fossil link to man is announced, there follows a debate marked by confusion about what was really found. Historically, for the hopeful evolutionists, it has become a big disappointment.

> The general public is rarely informed of the deep-seated uncertainty about human origins that is reflected in these statements by scientific experts. Instead, we are simply fed the latest version of somebody's theory, without being told that paleontologists themselves cannot agree over it. And

typically, the theory is illustrated with fanciful drawings of cave men, or human actors wearing heavy makeup.[1]

Missing links?

Ape-man fossils are rare and very expensive. They are often hidden away while castings, not the original bones of these ape-men, are sold and studied. Niles Eldredge of the American Museum of Science has said, regarding human evolution, that many scientists are removed from the actual data. Those in the inner circle who share a belief in evolution are permitted to view the actual fossil, while others are selectively censored.

But castings are no substitute for the real thing, particularly if they are to be studied in detail. The science of human evolution lacks openness. Science, by its nature, should be open to the scrutiny of other colleagues. This is not the case in the field of human evolution.

Whenever research access is selectively limited, scientific objectivity is impaired. Fossil specimens should be open to the public. Creationists should be free to examine them. Science has always been open to all and benefits from a wide range of opinions.

Evolutionary bias also infects the search for fossils. Darwinian presuppositions work effectively to exclude fossils that do not fit the evolutionary model and to selectively classify others. Human fossils have been downgraded to appear more ape-like, and ape fossils have been made to seem more human-like.

Alleged ape-men

Neandertal Man

French anthropologist Marcellin Boule published a series of scientific papers from 1911 to 1913, concluding that even though it had a larger brain size, Neandertal was closest to apes.

Boule, who found the most complete skeleton in Western Europe, ignored pathological evidence in the skeleton and assumed that the bones resembled an ape rather than a human. He concluded that his skeleton could not walk fully erect, but had bent knees and walked with his body leaning forward. He made the feet bend in, just like an ape's.

In 1955, two Americans noticed that there were some very serious problems with Boule's reconstruction. It took 44 years to expose the very obvious fact that Boule's Neandertal skeleton suffered from severe arthritis. After the corrections, Neandertal stood upright and walked like a human. Although it had, on average, a larger head than modern humans and a low cranium with heavy brow ridges, it was obviously human. Many believe that if Mr. Neandertal were waiting in a crowd at a bus stop today, we could not distinguish him from other humans. Numerous other lines of evidence support the full humanity of Neandertals, like the fact that they:

> Fossils of supposedly ape-like man are speculative, incomplete, falsified and imagined.

- had the technology to build fires, manufacture a high-tech superglue,[2] and construct stone-tipped spears[3]
- decorated their bodies with cosmetic pigments[4] and feathers[5]
- buried their dead[6]
- interbred with the ancestors of some people alive today (as shown by DNA analysis)[7]
- had anatomical[8] and genetic features[9] consistent with the capacity for speech.

Neandertal

For 44 years it was believed that the Neandertal man was an evolutionary predecessor to man—all because of Boule's enthusiastic fabrication. The popular idea of a brutish ape-like caveman has its origins not in the fossils, but in the mind of Boule. It can be seen now that Boule's motivation for his erroneous reconstruction was to indoctrinate the public into acceptance of evolution.

Despite the later correction, Boule's misrepresentation was not quickly removed. A life-size cave scene was drawn by famous artist Frederick Blaschke showing not one, but a whole family of

Neandertals. It became a permanent display and a very popular exhibition in the hall of the Chicago Field Museum of Natural History in the 1920s. This picture appeared in countless textbooks and other museums around the world. Amazingly, this cave scene stayed in the museum twenty years after it was disproved. Not only did this image linger on at the museum, it also remained for some time in textbooks and other museums around the world. This displayed an attitude that defied science and exposed the deep need to hold onto the evolutionary fantasy that humans evolved from brute beasts.

Piltdown Man

In Sussex, England, between 1908 and 1912, many parts of a human skull and two canine teeth were excavated, along with a primitive ape-like jaw. Significant parts of the upper and lower jaw were missing and the skull was in several parts. It was reconstructed, and castings were made and circulated to every major museum. There were other fossils found on the site, such as an elephant, mastodon, rhinoceros, hippopotamus, beaver, and deer.

The skull was called the 'Piltdown Man' and was considered a major find. It served for decades as proof of a link between man and his evolutionary ancestor. For 40 years, the authenticity of the fossil was widely accepted. In 1953, Kenneth Oakley, Joseph Weiner, and Wilfred Le Gros Clark exposed the skull as a fraud. The skullcap was actually fully human and the lower jaw fragments, including the teeth, were found in 1982 to be from a juvenile female orangutan. The jaw had been treated chemically to make it appear to match the skull.

It also should be noted that some of the mammalian bones found in that pit were planted and came from different areas, including the island of Malta and Tunisia. As early as 1916, there were reports of tampering, when dental anatomists noticed there were artificial abrasions on the teeth. These abrasions were clearly visible file marks on the orangutan's teeth. It was reported that in order for the lower jaw to fit the skull, the canine teeth were filed so far down that the pulp cavity was exposed and then plugged. The Piltdown hoax was mortifying to the evolutionary movement. It is no longer mentioned in textbooks, but it is clear that a desire remains to connect man with ape.

The closely held fashion in which human fossils are handled lends itself to fraud and exaggeration. The Piltdown skull was locked up in a vault, and very few could study it. Science is supposed to be self-correcting, and in this case, it took close to 40 years to expose the fraud. Perhaps if the vault had been left open, this could have been avoided.

Sadly, exclusivity still reigns today. With very few points of reference, given the overwhelming lack of fossils, there is enormous opportunity for creative interpretation and, given the lack of evidence, unscientific license.

Nebraska Man

In 1922, Harold Cook found a single molar tooth in Nebraska. It was identified by Henry Osborn, a paleontologist from the American Museum of Natural History, as belonging to an ape-man. Grafton Elliot Smith who was involved with the Piltdown hoax persuaded the prestigious *Illustrated London News* to publish an artist's conception of what this man and his mate might look like. It had to be drawn using one tooth.

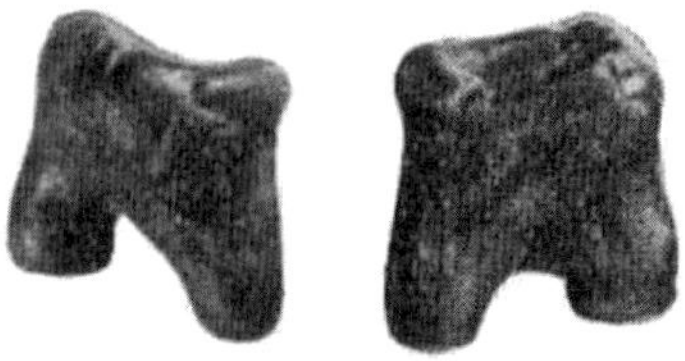

The 'Nebraska Man' tooth photographed from different angles

The magazine had worldwide distribution, and the illustration took two entire pages. It was published in June of 1922 and proclaimed as the 'missing link'. This illustration was firmly implanted in the public's mind during the famous Scopes 'Monkey Trial' in 1925. In 1928, the famous Nebraska man, based on a single tooth, came tumbling down. The tooth was discovered to be not that of an early man, but of an extinct pig. To add to the embarrassment, this 'extinct' pig was found in 1972 to be still alive in Paraguay.

Australopithecines (including 'Lucy')

The famous fossil 'Lucy' was found in Ethiopia by anthropologist Donald Johanson in 1974, and it was hailed as an intermediate link between humans and apes. Other fossils belonging to the same group (the australopithecines, meaning 'southern apes') have since been unearthed. But the Lucy skeleton is still the most complete of these, even though only 47 of its more than 200 total bones were recovered.[10]

The transitional status of Lucy's kind is based on the presumption that they walked upright. But the evidence is strongly against that idea. The australopithecines appear to be just extinct apes, and not on the path to become human, because they had the following combination of features:

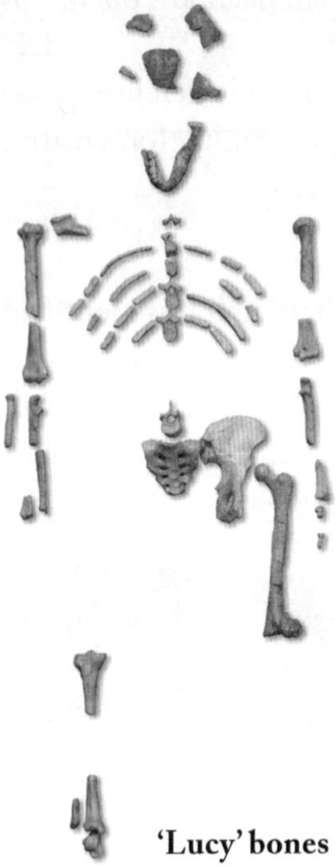

'Lucy' bones

*Cast of Lucy skeleton from *Museum national d'histoire naturelle*, Paris; photo by 120, Wikimedia Commons.

• A height of only about 1.1 meters (3 feet, 7 inches)
• A sloping, ape-like skull with a small braincase
• Muscular and highly curved fingers and toes for grasping tree branches[11]
• A locking-wrist mechanism used in knuckle-walking[12]
• An organ of balance in the inner-ear that was ape-like, not the kind for upright posture[13]

Still, evolutionists claim Lucy's kind walked upright because she had a slanted femur, bringing her knees close together for better balance. However, spider monkeys and orangutans also have this type of angled femur, and nobody claims they are the ancestors of humans. Also, a sophisticated anatomical study by evolutionist Dr Charles Oxnard concluded that: "The various australopithecines are, indeed, more different from both African apes and humans in most features than these latter are from each other."[14] In other words, the australopithecines were unique apes, not intermediate between humans and chimps.

Hobbits *(Homo floresiensis)*

In 2003, several miniature (just over 1 m tall) human skeletons were found on the Indonesian island of Flores. As usual, the discovery was interpreted through an evolutionary lens, and the 'Hobbits', as they were dubbed, were proclaimed to be an entirely different species of human that lived tens of thousands of years ago. However, many evolutionists themselves have argued that the fossils could be far younger, and they point to indications that the so-called Hobbits may have suffered from a disorder like microcephaly[15] or, in at least one case, Down syndrome.[16] In fact, it's likely that these individuals are the not-too-distant ancestors of the pygmies that live on the island today. In any case, the Hobbit skeletons lend no support to evolution, as evolutionist themselves cannot even come to a consensus about their significance.

Where are the ape-men?

Fossil bones that present evidence for a missing link, or ape-man, are extremely scarce. There is no clear body of evidence to support the claim that men descended from apes. The attempts made have a history of exaggeration and fraud.

Evolutionists do have a compelling reason to find fossil evidence of a transition from ape to man, but what has been found is either human or ape, not a missing link. Dr. Jonathan Wells, in his book *Icons of Evolution*, declares that the ultimate evolutionary icon is to show that man descended from apes. It is an attempt that, given the lack of evidence, is doomed to failure.

Wells cites Henry Gee, chief science writer for the prestigious science journal, *Nature*:

> To take a line of fossils and claim that they represent a lineage [from ape to man] is not a scientific hypothesis that can be tested, but an assertion that carries the same validity as a bedtime story—amusing, perhaps even instructive, but not scientific.[17]

Consequences of evolutionary beliefs

Racism

Darwin's *Origin of Species* is subtitled, *The Preservation of the Favored Races in the Struggle for Life*. Darwin's intent here was not racist, as the subtitle would seem to suggest. By the word 'races' he meant that all different species of animals would go through a gradual change through time, with natural selection.

However, in a later publication of *The Descent of Man*, he makes no excuses for what is an obviously racist idea, the effects of which would be felt well into the following century. Darwin states:

> At some future period, not very distant as measured by centuries, the civilized races of man will almost certainly exterminate, and replace, the savage races throughout the world. At the same time, the anthropomorphous apes … will no doubt be exterminated. The break between man and his nearest allies will then be wider, for it will intervene between man in a more civilized state, as we may hope, even than the Caucasian, and some ape as

> low as a baboon, instead of as now between the negro [sic] or Australian and the gorilla.[18]

The late Stephen Jay Gould, a prolific evangelist for evolution, acknowledged evolution's racist impact, stating,

> Biological arguments for racism may have been common before 1859, but they increased by orders of magnitude following the acceptance of evolutionary theory.[19]

One sad example of the racist fallout from Darwinism is the ill treatment of Ota Benga, a pygmy from central Africa. Benga, a 23-year-old male was placed in the Bronx Zoo in 1904 and displayed as an emblematic savage—an evolutionary ancestor who was encouraged to spend time in the monkey house. "Bushman shares a cage with Bronx Apes" was the *New York Times* headline on September 9, 1904.

Ota Benga

Francis Galton, the younger cousin of Charles Darwin, attempted to quantify human behavior. He insisted that intelligence correlated to moral behavior. Intelligence would lead to a moral life and vice versa. Galton believed that one's genetic endowment is the sole determinant of the entire gamut of human characteristics. Such thinking leads directly to the conclusion that some ethnic groups are superior to others. Galton also said that the gene pool should not be contaminated and therefore believed in the separation of the races.

"Judicious marriages" of "a certain stock" of human beings over "several consecutive generations" would produce a highly gifted race of people, according to Galton. This type of racism was called eugenics, which sought to create a superior race.

Ernst Haeckel (1834–1919), a German biologist who Darwin leaned on to prove evolution in the development of embryos, is remembered today for his forged illustrations of embryos. He also helped to make the case for legalized abortion by stating incorrectly that newborn infants are born deaf and without a conscience—which led to the idea that the newborn baby has no soul. So, what about the child inside the womb? Based on his logic, Haeckel said that abortion could not be considered murder. Haeckel was also strongly critical of the Bible for teaching racial equality, because he was a virulent white supremacist.[20]

Severe social consequences, such as racism, Nazism, and Communism follow when man substitutes evolution for the Creator.

Nazism

Many scholars have noted that Darwinian biology greatly influenced the thinking of Hitler. *Mein Kampf*, written in 1924 by Hitler, is evidence of this. Historian Werner Maser states:

> Darwin was the general source for Hitler's notions in biology, worship, force, struggle, and of his rejection of moral causality in history.[21]

Hitler was dedicated to an Aryan super-race and was directly influenced by the American publication of *The Passing of the Great Race* by the eugenicist Madison Grant, first published in 1916. "The Nazis extermination of six million 'racial undesirables' began with the quiet implication of Galton's eugenics."[22]

In Germany, Ernst Haeckel helped establish evolution as an intellectual and academic movement in Germany. It has been said that he shaped Darwinian evolution in Germany.

> Haeckelian Darwinism found its terroristic expression in national socialism. For Hitler, evolution was the hallmark of modern science and his "views of history, politics, religion, Christianity, nature, eugenics, science, art, and evolution, ... coincide for the most part with those of Haeckel." In the biological theory of Darwin, Hitler found his most powerful weapon against traditional values.[23]

> The German Führer, as I have consistently maintained, is an evolutionist; he has consciously sought to make the practice of Germany conform to the theory of evolution. He has failed, not because the theory of evolution is false, but because he had made three fatal blunders in its application.... First ... forcing the pace of evolution among his own people.... Second ... his misconception of the evolutionary value of power.... And the third (and greatest) mistake was his failure to realize that such a monopoly of

> power meant insecurity for Britain, Russia, and America. His three great antagonists, although they do not preach the doctrine of evolution, are very consistent exponents of its tenets.[24]

Evolution and communism

Karl Marx wanted to dedicate his *Das Kapital* to Darwin. Marx believed that Darwin's book contained the basic view of 'class struggle in history'. He read Darwin while in prison in December of 1860.

> Defending Darwin is nothing new for socialists. The socialist movement recognized Darwinism as an important element in its general world outlook right from the start. When Darwin published his *Origin of Species* in 1859, Karl Marx wrote a letter to Friedrich Engels in which he said, "... this is the book which contains the basis in natural history for our view."[25]

Joseph Stalin carried out the bloodiest massacres in world history by ordering the execution of 20 million people. He believed adamantly that the teaching of evolution would turn one against God and once God was removed, the people would be committed to the state. Pro-Stalin propaganda published in Moscow in 1940 illustrates this:

> "I'll lend you a book to read; it will show you that the world and all living things are quite different from what you imagine, and all this talk about God is sheer nonsense," Joseph [Stalin] said.
>
> "What book is that?" I enquired.
>
> "Darwin. You must read it," Joseph impressed on me.[26]

Different from the animals

It is ludicrous to assume that man is nothing else but an advanced form of animal. To see man as nothing but an intelligent life form can lead to unspeakable atrocities, as happened in the case of Nazism and communism. Evolution has sabotaged the intelligence of man with foolish thinking. Simple observation leads to the conclusion that there is a vast difference between animals and man.

So what makes humans different from animals? At least five observable characteristics: intelligence, language, creativity, moral conscience, and emotional depth. These illustrate the undeniable gulf between man and beasts.

> Man enjoys a special place in the created world.

Man's intelligence enables him to think abstractly and come to logical conclusions. Animals have varying degrees of intelligence, as observed in their behavior patterns. However, when one looks at what can be accomplished by man—solving complex mathematical equations, designing bridges, formulating solutions to complex problems, making scientific discoveries—it is obvious that the intelligence of animals is of a grossly inferior order. Can you imagine a monkey programming a computer with a complex language?

The capacity of humans to employ symbolic language is unique to man. There have been some advances with primates using language, and animals do have their own unique methods of communicating, such as a dolphin's sonar system. But while animals may use their senses to a higher degree, animal communication is not as complex as human language. Words and sentences have an abstract way of conveying concepts and information. Human language can convey enormous depth—as demonstrated by poetry, drama, and lyrics—and surpasses and is entirely distinct from animal language.

The creative capacity of man also distinguishes him from the animal kingdom. Humans have the ability to change and form things. They can use words, colors, sounds, symbols, tools and other things to form these elements into new expressions. The human face expresses within itself a uniqueness that can be identified from millions of other humans. No animal has the ability to form as many facial expressions as a human being.

Human hands, with opposable thumbs, have the ability to grasp and do fine detail work. Painting a picture, sculpting a statue, playing a musical instrument, singing a song, writing poetry, or even just a letter to a friend all reflect the unique creativity of man. Neither primates nor any other creature can creatively express themselves as can humans.

The ability to know right from wrong is truly human, and yet another marker dividing man from beast. There is, of course, trained behavior in which animals respond to a reward system. But this is no comparison to innate human moral consciousness. The legal system is an example of this difference. Justice for all, integrity, truthfulness, and honor are words that describe this phenomenon.

Evolutionists avoid this by blindly saying that over the years, man has gradually become aware of himself. They point out that this is an intellectual advancement due to evolutionary change. What the evolutionist fails to see is that this quality, the knowledge of good and evil, is deeply embedded in the spirit of man.

Humans, unlike animals, exhibit an enormous depth of emotion. The ability to feel pain, sorrow, love, or a thousand other emotions is much more intense with humans than with any other animal. This is true across the range of emotion—from horror to ecstasy. When a human smiles or frowns, he has the unique ability to externalize his emotional state. No creature on earth can experience so much emotional depth.

The human face, for example, is alone in the cosmos in its capacity to indicate fine degrees of emotion through a quarter million facial changes that are controlled by around 28 or more paper-thin muscles.[27] These facial changes are used to magnify emotional depth by expressing the character of one's human experience. This is unique to man.

Created in God's image

The evidence we have considered leads directly to the conclusion that all things—from molecule to man to the cosmos beyond—are the handiwork of a Creator of infinite intelligence. The heavens, the earth, all living organisms, including man, have characteristics that demonstrate order and design, a plan and a purpose. When, like a crime scene detective, one examines the physical evidence, the verdict is inescapable. It is just as Genesis declares: God did, indeed, create the heavens and the earth.

The random chaos that is the fundamental idea of evolution is altogether at odds with the rationality and design that we observe in creation. The mechanisms proposed for evolution do not square with the tenets of true science. Imagination, exaggeration, and in some cases, pure deception, are the hallmarks of the evolutionary movement.

Evolution has been advertised and marketed to the public as the only credible and intellectual explanation of the origins of the universe and all life. Many have accepted it without question because it has been dressed up with false scientific integrity. There are those, usually at the universities, who have zealously dogmatized the world with the canons of evolutionary thinking. They have become the priests in their own religion and work with an evangelistic energy to spread the faith of evolution. Yet this lie has had terrible practical consequences—among them abortion, Nazism, communism and different forms of socialism.

> Man was created in the image of God for the purpose of communion with his Creator.

Man is unique in the universe. He stands upright and is truly built for a noble purpose. The honest study of creation brings one to the inescapable sense that there is One far greater than we. That humbling realization also points to the fact that we are more than matter. We are not just body and mind, but creatures with a soul, who have been created in God's image to have a relationship and to commune with Him.

Jesus Christ, the *Logos* (Word), is the Creator, the one by whom "all things were created, in heaven and on earth, visible and invisible" (Colossians 1:16). Yet He became flesh and came down to make the ultimate sacrifice at Calvary. The death and resurrection of our Creator give us a new hope. It is solely by His grace, not of ourselves, that we can come to Him.

It is when the Spirit of our Creator God convicts us that we realize we are part of the Creator's plan. We simply cry out to Him in the realization of His great love for us, acknowledging that we are sinners and are willing to submit ourselves to the Creator, who is our Savior. If you have not already placed your faith in Jesus Christ, I urge you to do so—to meet your Maker, the One whose signature is engraved beyond question in the world He has made.

Notes

1. Jonathan Wells, *Icons of Evolution: Science and Myth*, Regnery Publishing, Washington, D.C., 2001, p. 225.
2. Neandertal superglue, *Creation* **24**(3):7, June 2002.
3. Michael Oard, Neandertal Man—the changing picture, *Creation* **25**(4):10–14, September 2003.

4. Robert W. Carter, The Painted Neandertal, 20 May 2010, creation.com/the-painted-neandertal.
5. Carl Wieland, Flights of Fancy, *Creation* **36**(4):19, October 2014.
6. Oard, Neandertal Man.
7. Robert W. Carter, Neandertal genome like ours, 01 June 2010, creation.com/neandertal-genome-like-ours.
8. Oard, Neandertal Man.
9. Peter Borger and Royal Truman, The FOXP2 gene supports Neandertals being fully human, *Journal of Creation* **22**(2):13–14, August 2008.
10. Russell Grigg, Are there apemen in your ancestry? *Creation* **25**(1)16–19, December 2002.
11. David Menton, Making man out of monkeys, 22 August 2000, creation.com/making-man-out-of-monkeys.
12. Michael Oard, Did Lucy walk upright? *Journal of Creation* **15**(2)9–10, August 2001.
13. Carl Wieland, Lucy: walking tall—or wandering in circles?, 22 July 2005, creation.com/lucy-walking-tall-or-wandering-in-circles.
14. 'Lucy' isn't the 'Missing Link'!, *Creation* **12**(3)32, June 1990.
15. Carl Wieland, Hobbit: New news is good news, 25 August, 2006, creation.com/hobbit-new-news-is-good-news.
16. David Klinghoffer, From PNAS, a Scathing Rebuke to Hype over *Homo Floresiensis*, Lost 'Hobbit' Species, 5 August, 2014, evolutionnews.org/2014/08/from_pnas_a_sca088671.html.
17. Wells, p. 221.
18. Charles Darwin, *The Descent of Man*, John Murray, London, 1901, pp. 241–242.
19. Stephen Jay Gould, *Ontogeny and Phylogeny*, Harvard University Press, Cambridge, Massachusetts, 1977, p. 127.
20. E. van Niekerk, Ernst Haeckel: a hostile witness to the truth of the Bible, 3 March 2011, creation.com/haeckel2.
21. Ian Taylor, *In the Minds of Men*, TFE Publishing, Toronto, Canada, 1987, p. 409.
22. Taylor, p. 410.
23. Kenneth J. Hsü, Sedimentary Petrology and Biologic Evolution, *Journal of*

Sedimentary Petrology, Vol. 56, September 1986, pp. 729–732.

24. Sir Arthur Keith, Evolution and Ethics, Putnam, New York, 1947, p. 230, quoted in Kenneth J. Hsü, Sedimentary Petrology and Biologic Evolution, *Journal of Sedimentary Petrology*, Vol. 56, September 1986.
25. Cliff Conner, Evolution vs. Creationism: In Defense of Scientific Thinking, *International Socialist Review*, Monthly Magazine Supplement to the *Militant*, November 1980.
26. E. Yaroslavsky, *Landmarks in the Life of Stalin*, Moscow: Foreign Languages Publishing House, 1940, pp. 8–12, vip.latnet.lv/LPRA/StalinsBrutal.htm#footnote1.
27. There is actually substantial variation in the number of face muscles between individuals, it is not uncommon to have 40 or more.

RECOMMENDED RESOURCES:

CREATION magazine

Keep your family informed on the latest easy-to-understand evidences for creation and against evolution. This unique full-colour family magazine gives God the glory, refutes evolution, and gives you the answers to defend your faith. Exciting material you won't find anywhere else! Includes a beautifully illustrated children's section in every issue. Powerful ammunition to intelligently discuss nature, history, science, the Bible, and related subjects. Quarterly magazine available as a paper and digital subscription.

EVOLUTION'S ACHILLES' HEELS

This powerful book (illustrated in full colour) exposes the fatal flaws of evolutionary thinking. Like no other work, it is authored by nine Ph.D. scientists to produce a coordinated, coherent, powerful argument. All of the authors received their doctorates from similar secular universities as their evolutionary counterparts. Each is a specialist in a field relevant to the subject addressed: Natural selection, origin of life, geology, genetics, radiometric dating, the fossil record, cosmology, and ethics.

THE CREATION ANSWERS BOOK

The Creation Answers Book provides biblical answers to over 60 important questions that everyone wants to know about creation/evolution and the Bible like "What about dinosaurs, carbon 14 dating, and who was Cain's wife?". Not only will it answer your questions, but it will equip you to effectively respond to the questions of others. This important work is a 'must have' for anyone's library.

WHY DOES A GOOD GOD ALLOW BAD THINGS? DVD

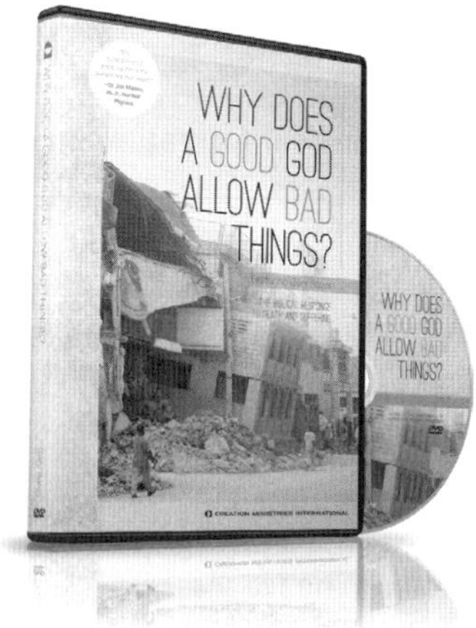

One of the most asked questions is why a loving God allows death and suffering. The heart of the Creator is revealed as Gary Bates persuasively unfolds the often overlooked issue in today's evolution-creation culture wars—the vital 'big picture' of the Gospel. Many hearts and minds were changed after hearing Gary explain the Gospel message with a powerful, yet compassionate approach.

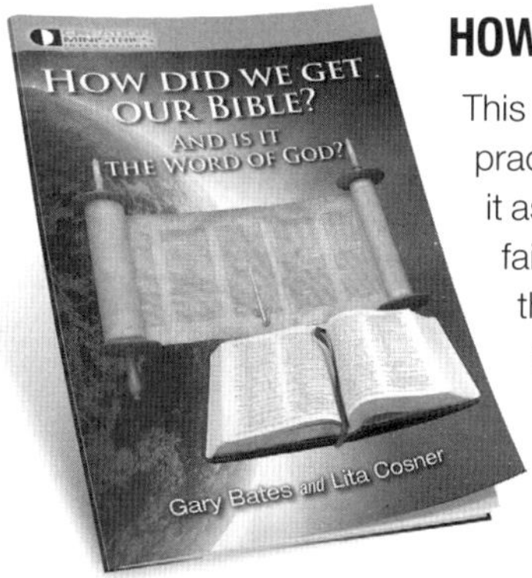

HOW DID WE GET OUR BIBLE? booklet

This 40-page booklet demonstrates historically and practically how the Bible came to be and why we can trust it as the Word of God. Christians will be encouraged in their faith by having adequate answers to defend their belief in the authority of Scripture. Along the way they will learn the ultimate reason why God chose to communicate with His creation. This booklet is ideal for those new in the faith and will also be suitable as a witnessing resource to non-believers.

THE AGE OF THE EARTH DVD

Many people think the earth is billions of years old. But geologist Dr Tas Walker shows that the evidence actually fits best with the biblical record of history. Dr Walker challenges us: How can we know the age of the earth? He shows why there is only one reliable way to know the age of anything—find out in this illustrated presentation. Includes English subtitles and a 3-minute CMI promotional segment.

CREATION.com

For more information on creation/evolution and Bible-science issues

AUSTRALIA
Creation Ministries International (Australia)
PO Box 4545
Eight Mile Plains, Qld 4113

Phone: (07) 3340 9888
Fax: (07) 3340 9889
ABN 31 010 120 304

CANADA
Creation Ministries International (Canada)
300 Mill St,
Unit 7, Kitchener, ON N2M 5G8

Phone: (519) 746–7616
Orders & donations: 1-888-251-5360
Fax: (519) 746–7617

NEW ZEALAND
Creation Ministries International (NZ)
PO Box 39005
Howick, Auckland 2145

Phone/Fax: (09) 537 4818
A Registered Charitable Trust

SINGAPORE
Creation Ministries International (Singapore)
Clementi Central Post Office
PO Box 195
Singapore 911207

Phone: 9698 4292

SOUTH AFRICA
Creation Ministries International (SA)
PO Box 3349
Durbanville 7551

Phone: (021) 979 0107
Fax: (086) 519 0555

UK & Europe
Creation Ministries International (UK/Europe)
15 Station St,
Whetstone, Leicestershire, LE8 6JS

Phone: 0116-2848-999

USA
Creation Ministries International (USA)
PO Box 350, Powder Springs,
GA 30127

Phone: 800-616-1264
Fax: (770) 439 9784

OTHER COUNTRIES
Creation Ministries International
PO Box 4545
Eight Mile Plains, Qld 4113
Australia

Phone: +617 3340 9888
Fax: +617 3340 9889